PRADA

PRADA TEL +44 207 399 2030

PRADA

In the first of a series of exclusive art projects Another Magazine sent British artist Jake Chapman to visit the newly opened Holy Land Experience in Orlando, Florida. New work by Jake and Dinos Chapman will be exhibited at The White Cube Gallery, London in early 2002.

THE HOLY LAND EXPERIENCE
Orlando, Florida, USA, Amen.
Dr Jake Chapman

IMAGES AND TEXT **JAKE CHAPMAN**
DESIGN **GARETH HAGUE** AT **ALIAS**

In the first of a series of exclusive art projects Another Magazine sent British artist Jake Chapman to visit the newly opened Holy Land Experience in Orlando, Florida. New work by Jake and Dinos Chapman will be exhibited at The White Cube Gallery, London in early 2002.

rom the airport take the Beeline Expressway 528 West to I-4 East. Follow the road for twenty minutes through Florida's lawn-mowed no-man's land, take Exit 31A and hang a left on Conroy Road. Do a right down Kirkman road until you hit International Drive. Here you'll find exits leading off the highway into the assemblage of pleasure-organs draped off Orlando's central cortex: Skull Kingdom™, Medieval Times®, Wet'n Wild®, Titanic, Ship of Dreams® and Planet Hollywood®. Or you might be drawn to the staple Universal Studios' Back to the Future™, Jurassic Park™ or Disney's Magic Kingdom®. Perhaps your pilgrimage to Orlando's theme-scape draws you *beyond the pleasure principle* in your quest to answer the really big questions: "Where did I come from? Why am I here? Where am I going? What is life really all about?" If so, turn off the I-4 exit ramp onto Vineland Road continuing for a few minutes passing fenced colonies of Greco-Roman condominiums until you reach a group of weathered columns on the right. Turn into the drive under the crumbling architrave. The sign reads: 'The Holy Land Experience™, Orlando'. Now you are entering into the *heart of lightness*. Cross the car park towards Jerusalem City Gate, which bares a perfect set of Floridian crenellations. At the ticket office you purchase a day pass, squeezing money though the vent in the bulletproof window to the polite lady inside who exchanges 'have a nice day, shalom and godbless' for $17.

You enter Holy Land by way of automated turnstiles, which nudge you towards the Old Scroll Shop and Methuselah's Mosaics. The street walls have an uncanny distemper: a burnt umber patina scumbled onto glass-fibre textures by busy Christians mimicking God's natural effects. Cartoon rendering bares plaster bricks - at any moment you expect Roadrunner to beep beep past. Instead an old woman stationed at the end of the passage, dressed in pantomime Hessian, lightly strums a King David's harp practising for the afterlife. She has a Christian smile and backlit eyes. You would like to help her on her way.

Opening out onto the Via Dolorosa Path looking beyond the current of motile visitors and their pet wheelchairs, stands mini-Calvary with three wooden crucifixes branded into the hot Orlando sky. Visitors congregate here paralysed by the sight of the cross - halted by the symbolic

*THE SCRIPTORIUM:
CENTER FOR BIBLICAL ANTIQUITIES
*OPENING EARLY 2002

The Holy Land EXPERIENCE
ORLANDO

THE B
CA

OASIS LAGOON

OASIS
PROMENADE

S
E

THE JERUSALEM STREET MARKET
- A Jerusalem City Gate
- B Ticket Center
- C Guest Services
- D Restrooms
- E The Old Scroll Shop
- F Methuselah's Mosaics
- G The Sycamore Tree
  Proprietor: Zacchaeus

CALVARY'S GARDEN TOMB
- H Via Dolorosa Path
- I Millstone Garden

THE QUMRAN DEAD SEA CAVES

THE WILDERNESS TABERNACLE
- J Bedouin Tent Queue

OASIS PALMS CAFE

THE PLAZA OF THE NATIONS
- K The Nicanor Stage: *Live music and drama throughout the day*

THE TEMPLE OF THE GREAT KING

THEATER OF LIFE:
Now showing: **The Seed of Promise**

THE BYZANTINE CARDO

THE JERUSALEM MODEL A.D. 66
Live presentations throughout the day

*THE SCRIPTORIUM:
CENTER FOR BIBLICAL ANTIQUITIES
*Opening Early 2002

THE JERUSALEM MODEL A.D. 66

THE TEMPLE OF THE GREAT KING

NTINE O

I-4 EAST TO DOWNTOWN ORLANDO

THEATER OF LIFE

4

I-4 WEST TO AREA ATTRACTIONS

K

THE PLAZA OF THE NATIONS

OASIS PALMS CAFE

THE WILDERNESS TABERNACLE

I-4 EXIT 31A

CALVARY'S GARDEN TOMB

THE QUMRAN DEAD SEA CAVES

J

E

I

H

F

ONAL BITS

D

G

C

A

B

THE JERUSALEM STREET MARKET

magnitude of Christ's death reduced to human proportion, to a profane stage set. Behind the empty crosses, the sound of a nail being driven by a hammer draws you round the base of Calvary's mound engendering infected images of its steel point piercing through a wrist into wood. Reaching the other side a gardener drives a tent pin into the earth not more than fifteen feet away from the cross. The vertiginous proximity between nail and cross cannot fail to incite reflex burps of diabolic laughter to rise from your duodenum.

You walk past a rock discarded by the wayside, its phenomenological deceit jumps out at you hissing piped music, which swirls in the background in perpetual crescendo. Much as Christ's resolve was tested and mocked by Satan's hallucinations in the desert, your reality drips and distorts with cheap cinematics underscoring the fallacious nature of each facet of Holy Land's ham-fisted (kosher) phenomena. Only the viewfinder can smooth the seams and jumps, restore filmic continuity to the props and sets, which detain verisimilitude from working properly for the naked eye. True enough, the cinematic soon erupts into action. Booming through the P.A. a woman's voice urgently informs us she has *seen the one they call Jesus Christ.* The crowd is confused - they haven't, and if they don't soon they'll demand their money back. The voice tumbles from speech into song, drawling and imploring, forming the words through a falsetto orifice which does the song no favours; 'He loves you... and you... and you, and you... and *me!*'

Her voice is desiccated with heartfelt emotion each day at two-thirty sharp, so you zoom-in to snatch a better look and see she's a bit like the Virgin Mary with make-up. Other members of the cast assemble, pushing through the crowd making us feel like we're *really there, a part of the crowd.* Melodies lattice together with the backing track. *Madonna's* radio-mic battles with the feedback bouncing from the Tomb's black hole gaping behind. Without warning the crowd bifurcates in panic to allow a half-naked man covered in vermilion blood to struggle with a single beam of wood to which he is chained and is carrying across his shoulders. Three or four Roman soldiers bait him with plastic whips, ordering him on in harsh Sparticus tones. The crowd is *genuinely* shocked, confused about how to react. Looking around for direction they appear ashamed in their calculation, unsettled in their fear and indecision. Pathos confuses the division between the territory of spectator and the tortured body, an instant of abreactive trauma that fails to excite reflex compassion. The crowd is paralysed, a patent lapse of Samaritan altruism left begging in the simulacrum of Christ, stumbling and bleeding before their eyes. This is how the Second Coming will be: you can see he is Christ, you can appreciate his pain, yet still you do nothing! Do we need to kill him twice? Yes. Perhaps more.

He does not drag a crucifix, and so false idolatry has been avoided. This is only a *sort-of-Jesus*: a figural stunt man transfixing us in the facsimile spectacle that transports us to the moment of Mankind's ignoble betrayal.

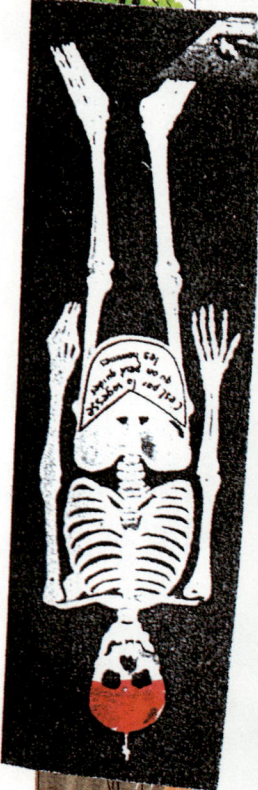

Disposable cameras soon continue to wink at the drama, collecting scenes for print technicians in photo bureaus all over America to puzzle over once the process has congealed a semblance of reality in photographic catalysis.

Christ continues along Via Dolorosa Path as Virgin Mary climaxes. The Lord reappears reconstituted in a white shroud, risen defiant on the brow of Calvary to release a snow white dove, which flies away into the blue sky (making a circuit of the Holy Land to return to its coop in the service area). Lightly traumatised, the lapsed Christians disassemble, meandering off toward the Wilderness Tabernacle, the Temple of the Great King, the Qumran Dead Sea Caves or the Oasis café.

Over-stretched grins bear polished enamel tombstones on faces whose capillaries have dried out, vessels don't vascularise anymore and blusher does the job of representing life where sullen grey parchment falls shrink-wrapped into skeletal cavities. Christian Die-hards can expect eternity in the Kingdom of God but cling to the last quiver of gelatinous life nonetheless, betraying the material substance of their skepticism.

The *terminal* merge with the old-aged, putting a brave face-lift on the inexorable influence of gravity, entropy and the shit-filled coffin waiting to lap them up. The cellulitic amass in swarms, their folds flock to the Holy Land to lay their *big-boned* limbs upon the Lamb of Christ and tear warm flesh from its tiny lickle bones. In the 'Oasis Palms cafe' obese diners declare a Fatwah upon food, stuffing David and Goliath burgers into their swollen holes and expelling its

allegorical meat as de-consecrated excrement. *'This is my body. This is my blood. This is the restroom'.*

It's hard not to assume a complexity backslide occurring with each successive generation of Christian progeny, imagining these organisms devolving back into the waters of Holy Land's own ornamental pond, all of them merging together into the blubbering bioflesh of a colossal Jonah's whale.

'Do you think this is *like* the Holy Land - *like* Israel?' I ask a grazing Christian.

'Israel? Is that *out* of the country?'

Necrophobia reeks from the sand, prehistoric silicate-crustacia ground down by the abrasive sandal shuffle of the procession of the damned, the lemming waves of mortal humans terrified of leaping the synaptic chasm between their final breath and everlasting life. Still they smile. As they sink they smile. As I drown one of them in the shallow end of the Oasis Lagoon's gene pool they smile, gurgling 'have a nice day, shalom and godbless!'

The Christian smile is the iconic embodiment of disingenuity. The impervious face that smiles its sublime symmetry through all seasons: loathing body-horror, phobic hatred and fear. Banal politeness is suppressed violence hidden by the special effects of a *service language* that calculates aggressivity out of its formal permutations. Have a nice day. Shalom. Godbless. The *willingness to please* and *be nice* conspires its endosymbiotic absorption, a technique that dissolves difference and treats it as diseased hostility. *Love thy neighbour as you love thyself* asserts

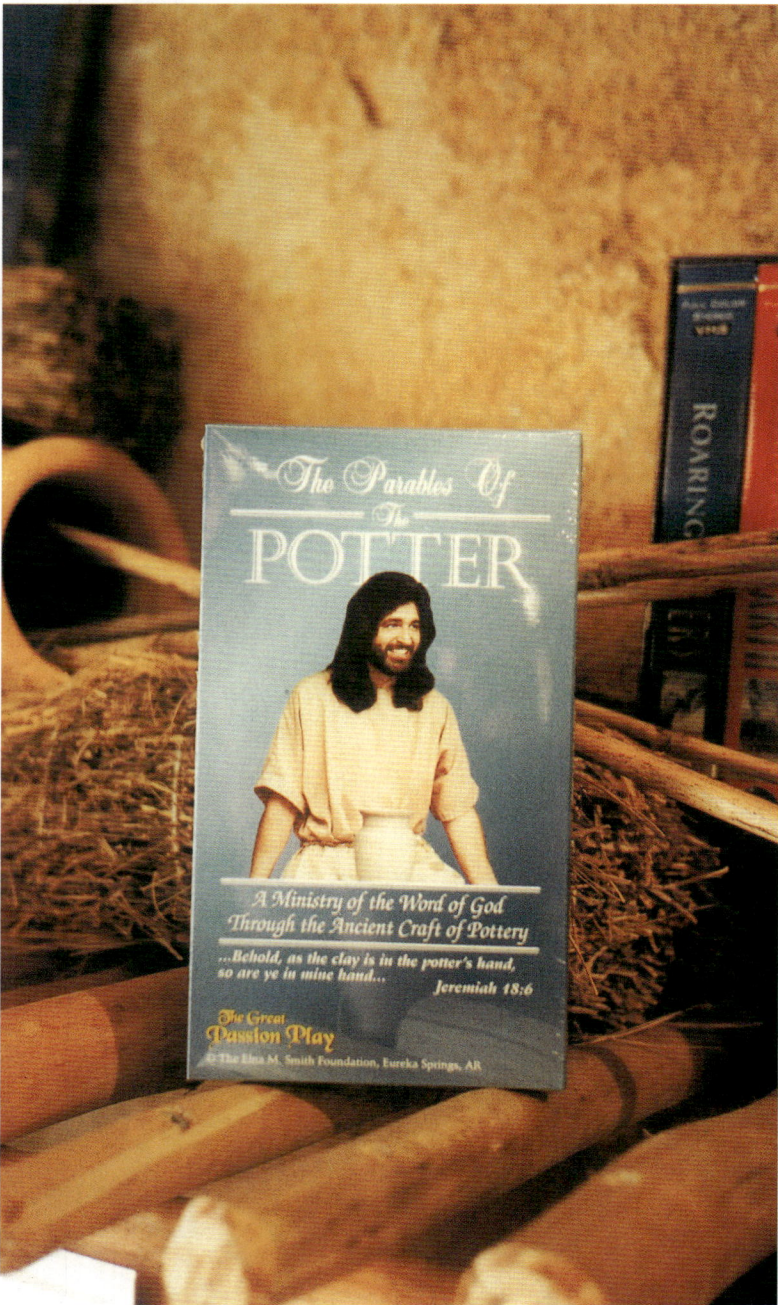

The Parables Of
The
POTTER

A Ministry of the Word of God
Through the Ancient Craft of Pottery

...Behold, as the clay is in the potter's hand,
so are ye in mine hand...
Jeremiah 18:6

The Great
Passion Play
© The Elna M. Smith Foundation, Eureka Springs, AR

similarity as the means by which otherness must be conceived. However much you berate the fuckers they feel sorry for you, a metabolic adaption that energises their resource for piety and masochistic self-satisfaction.

Financial impropriety takes you straight to hell. This is the message of the cul-de-sac missionaries whose own culture and identity was obliterated and replaced with simplistic colonial monotheism sold by exiles and malaria-ridden drunks. Now the *return of the repressed* visit our atheistic shores laden with 'Watchtower' magazines, leisure-time religions and simplistic flexitime faith. Aristocratic theology is made redundant where Old Testament parables are taken as truth by plebiscite blue-colour ministers. Evangelist descriptions of life *after* death are always a little like life *before* death but divinely transubstantiated into wish-fulfilled hyper-reality: where the celestial light of New-God dissolves domestic, racial, class and gender disparities: beneficent Nature sees lambs and lions lying together while predation is calculated out of the food chain altogether. These religions blossom from the trepidations of credit culture, from the Faith required to take out yet another loan, to stack more interest upon teetering mortgages - from living life on the *never never* which is purgatory absolute: *Remember*, Satan says in the small print, *deferring on credit repayment will break your contract with everlasting life in the Kingdom of God.*

Evangelist rewards offer life beyond entropy, transcending sell-by-dates like the polyurethane material of Mastercard or American Express, never eroding in the vicissitudes of time, and will, I'm afraid, outstrip your flesh.

In Holy Land's Jerusalem Model A.D 66, a modestly suited door-to-door missionary with the charisma of doG shit stands erect in the middle of a large diorama pointing a laser cursor at significant waypoints on the road to Calvary. He lectures at speed, a blitzkrieg delivery obliterating detail in the summation of the totalised effect - a mesmeric mantra accelerating past Pontious Pilate's taciturn interest in Christ's adjudication and only decelerating at the explanation of the *slaughter of the lamb*. And why? 'The sinner lays his hands upon the innocent body of the lamb', he says, subliminally infected by the feverish manner of Robert Mitchum in Night of the Hunter. 'Sin passes from his sinner's hands into the very body of the innocent lamb, who absorbing his sin must be ritually sacrificed. This, my friends, is our debit to the Lord Jesus Christ, who sacrificed himself for us, the Lamb of God, Amex'.

'Amen', reflect the puce faces of the triple mortgaged, the bankrupt and lonesharked, finding momentary repose in his words, as though a sinner's hands had been lifted from their lamb-like shoulders.

Slaughter in Orlando's Holy Land comes expected in the form of the hard-ish sell, even though the figural rewards of redemption are merchandised in the same material terms condemned as the 'base materiality' of life *before* Testimony. Covetousness is next to commodityness. The gift-shop sells the core-theme of

death-terror: each dollar spent is a laser waypoint on the path to final judgement and everlasting life. Slimline Bibles for obese motherfuckers, creative literature explaining DNA, molecular physics and dinosaurs within the possessive axioms of Christianity, a diffusion range of Holy Land Experience logo-apparel emblazoned on hats T-shirts and sweaters and parables of goodness in digital and analogue form - anything to trade on the fear of maggots.

Christianity fatigue has clearly fogged the memory. It was once well served by the virulent annihilations of the Crusaders and sublime violence of Giles de Rais: inquisitors and vehement martyrs whose tendency toward tragic redemption, bloodthirsty retribution and the destructive wastage of surplus wealth made Faith an act of absolute obeisance witnessed in the communion of blood. Christianity was never a religion of *charity* or calculation - its beneficence was, as Marcel Mauss suggests, conceived as an un-returnable gift, as a potlatch, which locked the recipient forever in debt. As far as God is concerned Christ's death is un-returnable for mankind, marking the resentment with which Humanism sought to overturn the obligation.

Liberal fundamentalism takes pleasure in vivisecting religion in the course of flexing its sentimental cynicism (often unaware that it is also deriving its values from a monotheistic heritage). Heroic existentialism inherits its avant-garde tenure from the image of Judaeo-Christianity's divine Omnipotent - the One formed in radical solitude. This singularity is reconfigured in the secularisation of the Christian psyche in psychoanalysis, where schizoid polytheism is pathologised in the humanist creed elaborating its unholy trinity in the hypocritical unity of the id, ego, and superego.

One last thing. Charities collect money to afford terminally ill children a temporary exodus to Disney land, faithful that the excesses of velocity and vertigo will for an instant compensate the shit-end-of-the-stick they were born to lean on. There are no rides in The Holy Land Experience other than the merry-go-round of wheelchairs perambulating the terminally ill around the mean *trompe l'oeil* sets as though a vestige of relief can be gleaned from the illusory one-dimensional. In Holy Land the semiotics of greed impound every surface in a general economy of priced utility and nothing can abrogate itself from this greedy nihilism. Contempt is easy and the tendency to Christian-baiting discloses no fresh sport.

If you exit the Holy Land Experience, past the weathered Roman columns, taking a left down Vineland Road toward Kirkman Road, hang a left toward Universal Drive, you will come to Universal Studios. In the massive Universal complex you will see the Hard Rock Colosseum building - partially ruined by a fake lava-flow of pyroclastic rock with a pink Chevrolet oyster embedded in its bulk. The entire Holy Land Experience would fit comfortably inside the Colosseum with room to spare. And with the addition of some emaciated lions Orlando would *really* have an attraction.

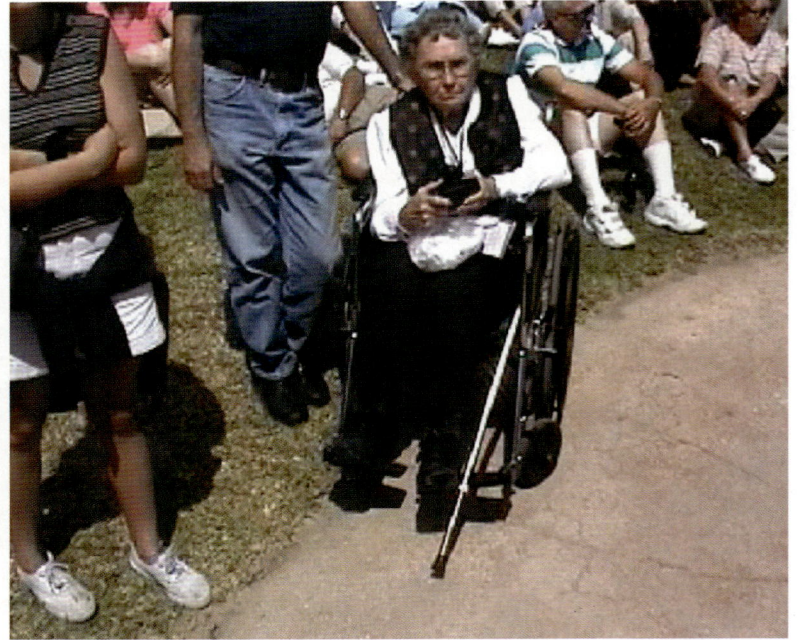

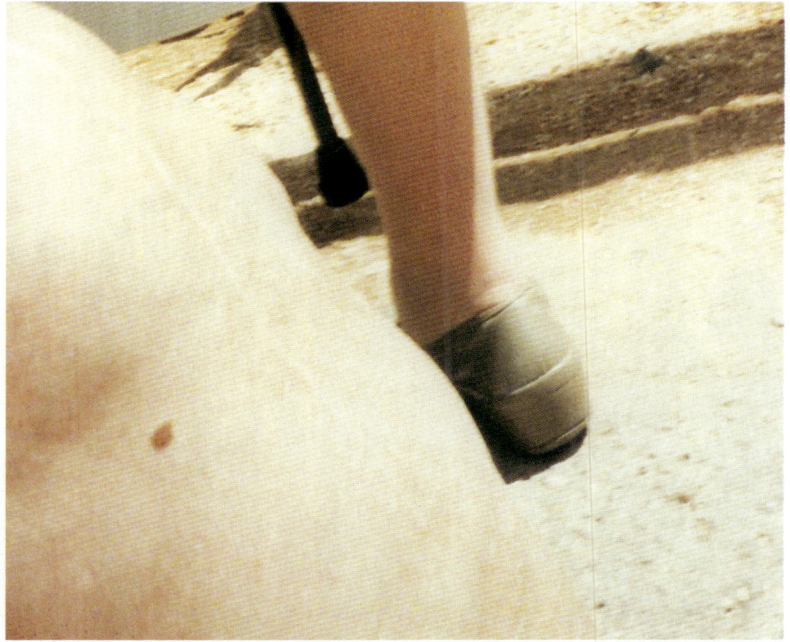

DUSTIN AND ANNE BYNE, CANNES, 1977

PHOTOGRAPHED BY DANIEL ANGELI. COPYRIGHT DANIEL ANGELI/ALPHA

Arriving at Nice airport on route to the Cannes Film Festival Dustin Hoffman recognises the veteran gentleman paparazzo Daniel Angeli and adopts a Python-esque silly walk to accentuate the difference in height between himself and his spouse.

ISSUE 1

ANOTHER MAGAZINE FOR MEN AND WOMEN AUTUMN/WINTER 2001

FASHION

PERFORMANCE

SOUL WINDOWS

CENTREFOLD

KATE HUDSON & CHRIS ROBINSON

INTERVIEWS

GUCCI

GUCCI

CONTENT 2\2

COVER: ZORA AND OLIVIER WEAR MIU MIU AND DOUGLAS DAY ASCENCIO, PHOTOGRAPHED BY **NICK KNIGHT**, STYLED BY **KATY ENGLAND** AND RETOUCHED BY **ALLAN FINAMORE**.

FLORAL DANCE, LOS ANGELES, 1978

PHOTOGRAPHED BY HENRY GRIS. COPYRIGHT CAMERA PRESS
Clint Eastwood watches his wife Maggie Johnson modelling a swimsuit in their Hollywood home
at the time he was filming Every Which Way But Loose. Eastwood has been married twice
since. His current wife is Dina Ruiz; 35 years his junior, they have a five year old daughter.

Dior

BURBERRY

NEW BOND STREET 020 7839 5222

BURBERRY

NEW BOND STREET 020 7839 5222

MASTHEAD

EDITOR IN CHIEF **JEFFERSON HACK**
CREATIVE DIRECTOR **ALEX WIEDERIN** AT **AR MEDIA**

FASHION
FASHION DIRECTOR **KATY ENGLAND**
SENIOR FASHION EDITORS **SABINA SCHREDER, ALISTER MACKIE**
CONTRIBUTING FASHION EDITORS **TABITHA SIMMONS, CAMILLA NICKERSON, NANCY ROHDE**
SENIOR FASHION FEATURES EDITOR **SUSANNAH FRANKEL**
FASHION EDITOR **SOPHIA DE ROMARATE** sophia@anothermag.com
FASHION COORDINATION **JO HAMMOND** jo@anothermag.com

PHOTOGRAPHY
PHOTOGRAPHIC DIRECTOR **EMMA REEVES** emma@anothermag.com
ASSISTANT PHOTOGRAPHIC EDITOR **JAM**
PHOTOGRAPHY INTERN **CLARKE TOLTON**

FEATURES
SENIOR EDITOR **MARK SANDERS** mark@anothermag.com
DEPUTY EDITOR **EDWARD HELMORE** edward@anothermag.com
CONTRIBUTING EDITOR **NEVILLE WAKEFIELD** neville@anothermag.com
LITERARY EDITOR **DAN CROWE** dan.crowe@anothermag.com
EDITORIAL ASSISTANT **KATE EMELIANOVA** kate@anothermag.com

DESIGN
JUNIOR ART DIRECTOR **THOMAS HOFER** thomash@ar-media.com
DESIGNER **NOBI KASHIWAGI** nobik@ar-media.com

TEXT
DAVE CALHOUN, HELEN CASTLE, JAKE CHAPMAN, YOLANDA EDWARDS, KATE EMILIANOVA, EMMA E FORREST, SUSANNAH FRANKEL, EDWARD HELMORE, BARNEY HOSKYNS, WENDY IDE, CALLUM MCGEOCH, ROGER MORTON, ALISON POWELL, BRUCE ROBINSON, MARK SANDERS

PICTURES
PIERRE BAILLY, FIONA BANNER, MARK BORTHWICK, CEDRIC BUCHET, RICHARD BURBRIDGE, THOMAS C CARD, JAKE CHAPMAN, PHILIP LORCA DICORCIA, HORST DIEKGERDES, MICHAEL EVANET, HUGER FOOTE, MAURIZIO GUILLEN, ALEXEI HAY, OLIVER HELBIG, MATT HOLYOAK, BERT HOUBRECHTS, ERIC JOHNSON, GREG KADEL, MARCELO KRASILCIC, NICK KNIGHT, CHRIS MOORE, HELMUT NEWTON, TOBIAS NILSSON, PERRY OGDEN, ROBERT POLIDORI, PHIL POYNTER, TERRY RICHARDSON, WILLIAM SELDEN, DAVID SIMS, MARIO SORRENTI, VANINA SORRENTI, JOEL STERNFELD, DANIEL STIER, JUERGEN TELLER, MATTHIAS VRIENS, NICK WAPLINGTON, GUY WENBORNE, JUSTIN WESTOVER, KURT DE WIT

ADVERTISING
UNITED KINGDOM: SENIOR FASHION ADVERTISING MANAGER **ROB MONTGOMERY**
+44 (0) 20 7549 6826 rob@anothermag.com
GROUP ADVERTISING MANAGER **CHRISTOPHER LOCKWOOD**
+44 (0) 20 7549 6829 christopher@anothermag.com
FASHION ADVERTISING EXECUTIVE **BETTY DEMONTE** +44 (0) 20 7549 6850 betty@anothermag.com
ADVERTISING EXECUTIVES **TIM FLEMING** +44 (0) 20 7549 6848 tim@anothermag.com,
ED SEARLE +44 (0) 20 7549 6806 ed@anothermag.com
ITALY: JEFFREY BYRNES JB Media +39 02 2901 3427 jbmedia@tin.it Fax: +39 02 2901 3491
FRANCE: GERALDINE POSTEL Outcasts Inc. +33 (0)1 48 06 99 98 geraldine_outcasts@noos.fr
Fax: +33 (0)1 48 06 99 98

SPONSORSHIP
GROUP COMMERCIAL DIRECTOR **ANDREW KING** +44 (0) 20 7336 8272 andrew@anothermag.com
SENIOR ADVERTISING & SPONSORSHIP EXECUTIVE **FAYE ANTHONY** +44 (0) 20 7549 6832
faye@anothermag.com
For individual creative projects, please contact ANOTHER MAGAZINE promotional and sponsorship
team on +44 (0) 207 336 8272 or +44 (0) 207 549 6826.
UK · ANDREW KING +44 (0) 207 336 8272 andy@anothermag.com & **ROB MONTGOMERY**
+44 (0) 207 549 6826 rob@anothermag.com Fax: +44 (0) 20 7549 6860

MARKETING & PR
GROUP MARKETING, EVENTS & PR MANAGER **NICKI BIDDER** +44 (0) 207 549 6821
UNITED KINGDOM: GILLIAN MCVEY PURPLE PR +44 (0) 207 439 9888 gillian@purplepr.com
USA: KERRY YOUMANS KCD +44 (0) 212 590 5100 youmans@kcdworld.com

REPRO: AJD COLOUR +44 (0) 207 987 3220
RETOUCHING: THE SHOEMAKERS ELVES +44 (0) 207 490 3235
PRINTING: NATIONAL PRESS, JORDAN +962 (6) 420 00 21

PRODUCTION
GROUP PRODUCTION DIRECTOR **STEVEN SAVIGEAR** steve@anothermag.com
MANAGING EDITOR **LOTTE OULD** lotte@anothermag.com
PRODUCTION EDITOR **AMY SLATTER** amy@anothermag.com
PRODUCTION MANAGERS **NIKKI TAYLOR & DAVID CORBETT** david@anothermag.com
SUB EDITORS **ALEX CASSELL & ROB MORGAN**

CIRCULATION
SENIOR DISTRIBUTION MANAGER **STUART WHITE** stuart@anothermag.com

PUBLISHING
PUBLISHERS **JEFFERSON HACK, RANKIN WADDELL**
PUBLISHING DIRECTOR **SUSANNE WADDELL** susanne@anothermag.com
CHIEF OPERATING OFFICER **RONNY LEACH** ronny@anothermag.com
GROUP OFFICE MANAGER **LIAM KELLY** liam@anothermag.com
FINANCIAL CONTROLLER **NATALIE SMITH** natalie@anothermag.com
FRONT DESK **BECKY RAWLINSON** becky@anothermag.com

SUBSCRIPTION
Please write your name and address on the back of the cheque or postal order.
UK, EUROPE & REST OF THE WORLD:
ANOTHER MAGAZINE, PO BOX 1079, Wallington, SM5 4SQ
Enquiries +44 (0) 20 8669 5561 another@optimumltd.co.uk
USA, CANADA & SOUTH AMERICA:
ANOTHER MAGAZINE, International media service, 3330 Pacific Avenue, Suite 404, Virgina
Beach, VA 23451 2983 USA. Enquiries +1 757 428 8180 imsnews@visi.net

ANNUAL SUBSCRIPTION: UK £25, EUROPE £35, REST OF WORLD £45, AMERICAS $50

Special thanks to
Jim Moffat, Ed Filipowski, Kate Moss, Mario Sorrenti, Pascal Dangin, Alex Gonzales, Raul Martinez,
Michelle Gaillard-Fuertes, Art Tavee, Francois Ravard, Simon Halls, Philipp Haemmerle, Charlotte
Knight, Val Williams, Mesh Chhibber, Roy & Anne Waddell, Alex Betts, Harbottle & Lewis, Daniel
Irons, Beatrice Novobaczky, John Langston, Jenny Koo, Maco Kusunoki, Richard Austin, Mandie
Erickson, Kate Comegys
Another Magazine would like to acknowledge Peter Friedrichs as the original designer of Magnificat.

JACK'S ASS, ST TROPEZ, 1976

PHOTOGRAPHED BY DANIEL ANGELI. COPYRIGHT DANIEL ANGELI/ALPHA

Accompanied by producer Sam Spiegel (with back to camera), his old friend, the pop impresario Lou Adler (left) and his girlfriend, Jack Nicholson provides a polite diversion for the day-tripping Cannes paparazzi. Spiegel and Nicholson were on the Riviera to promote Harold Pinter's screen adaptation of F Scott Fitzgerald's novel, The Last Tycoon, starring Robert de Niro in the title role. But it was another de Niro title role that took home the Palme d'Or, Martin Scorcese's Taxi Driver.

Ready-to-wear, Shoes, Leather Goods. Sold exclusively
in Louis Vuitton stores. http://www.vuitton.com

LOUIS VUITTON

Chloé

FORWARD

Another Magazine: another point of intervention, another set of discoveries, another way of looking at things, another 30 minutes of your time, another kiss, another curious idea that just came to mind, another reason to get out of bed in the morning, another sense of déjà vu, another chance to do it all over again next season. Another damn fine day.

We wish our lives to be less complicated and more spiritually rewarding yet we are creatures of extremes. Taken to habit and spurred by random acts of chaos. We laugh when we should cry and make others cry when we should make them happy. We are silly and smart, selfish and caring, the modern metaphysical children of Adam and Eve. This is our Original Sin. Our humanity, our right to fuck up and pick up the pieces. To learn as we go along and make the same mistakes again. To lose ourselves in the moment and put things off for another day.

Another Magazine explores these themes through the writing, fashion, photography and vision of its contributors. The cover of this issue by Nick Knight shows two young lovers in a personal embrace. To show real love, in a real situation with real people is something few contemporary magazines would attempt or even think to do. That's our cover statement for this season: to keep a sense of romance alive in a world where ideals are often replaced by deals, and desire easily subverted by greed. It is about an attitude that carries through the fashion and literature to influence and effect contemporary thinking. There is little time in our culture to allow surprises, radical ideas and thoughts to emerge. We are moving, consuming and communicating so fast that it takes real control to slow down rather than just go with the flow. Recessions, wars, global and personal disasters continue, and often lives remain uninterrupted. As our culture accelerates and people jump on the latest money-go-round, we see a uniformity of opinions and ideas, a homogenisation of theories, images and fashion. It's as if the faster things become the smaller the sphere of reference revealed.

Another Magazine is not going to change the world we live in. It exists to expand that sphere of reference, to show that there is more to our lifestyles than the obvious. That there is a need to slow down and assess, as much as there is a desire for constant entertainment. Another Magazine juxtaposes these extremes in a magazine "for men and women", a magazine "for people".

Art directed in New York and produced in London, Another Magazine traverses a continental style divide. Its writers and photographers come from all over the world. Some of them are visionaries whose names you may recognise others are emergent protagonists in the media landscape. These are our protagonists; producing images you will want to rip out and stick on your wall, articles you will want to highlight and keep to re-read. They have come together to fire inspiration and action, style and reflection into the ether; to kick through our daily realities and fuel the fantasies of a generation caught in the slipstream of the extreme.

Jefferson Hack
Editor-in-Chief

YVES SAINT LAURENT
■ *rive gauche* ■

YVES SAINT LAURENT

■ *rive gauche* ■

DOLCE & GABBANA

VALENTINO

PHONE 020 78386288

20-22 SLOANE STREET

FENDI

+39 06 334501

ANOTHER THING I wanted to tell you

ANOTHER MAGAZINE ASKS TWELVE VISIONARIES TO GET PERSONAL AND SHARE A PASSION WITH US. WHAT ARE THEY THINKING ABOUT, LISTENING TO, READING ABOUT OR SEARCHING FOR RIGHT NOW?

AIMEE MULLINS VITALITY
CHRISTINE VACHON DOLLS
NOEL GODIN ANARCHY
CHAN MARSHAL EARTH
HAL WILNER LAUGHTER
ROMAN COPPOLA FUTURISM
KIM GORDON VOICE
BRUCE MAU AMERICA
BENEDIKT TASCHEN DIRECTION
CHRIS OFILI BEATS
SIMON DOONAN TASTE
TERRY GILLIAM TIME
KARYN KUSAMA WAR

ANOTHER THING I Wanted To Tell You
by Aimee Mullins, Athlete and model

A balance between the mind and body, as exemplified by Pilates.

"'ve been practising Pilates for years and I recently got a book to try some moves while I was on the road travelling. I like that Pilates comprises the mind and the body. It's not just about being able to run around the block a few times. It's about alleviating stress and controlling breathing. It's about being balanced. If you're an athlete and you completely focus on the body you're missing other components. Similarly, if you're trying to broaden your mind but not also being attentive to your sense of humour and your spirit, then you're not going to grow and develop so fast. When reading, I take the philosophy that I'll be reading one book that is provoking the intellect - I'm reading the writings of Indira Gandhi at the moment - and then something for the body and the spirit. I also read something for the funny bone, some-

thing completely ridiculous, with no self-betterment in mind at all!"

Born without fibula bones, 25-year-old athlete and model Aimee Mullins had both legs amputated below the knees when she was young. After entering athletic competitions at Georgetown University, she now holds records in the 100 metres, 200 metres and long jump events; and competed at the '96 paralympics in Atlanta. Aimee now runs long distance too, recently competing in a two kilometre charity race in New York's Central Park ("I couldn't feel my shoulders!"). As well as modelling and travelling to India, where she spoke on the subject of landmines and prosthetic limbs at the Women's Medical College, Aimee has spent recent months acting in an art film set to be released next year.

PILATES IS PRACTISED AT THE **MACKENZIE CHAMBERS STUDIO**, NEW YORK 001 646 613 8410

AIMEE MULLINS PHOTOGRAPHED BY **GREG KADEL** IN BROOKLYN. TEXT BY **DAVE CALHOUN**

ANTEPRIMA

ANOTHER THING I Wanted To Tell You

by Christine Vachon, Film Producer

Superstar: The Karen Carpenter Story, a short film by Todd Haynes using Barbie dolls.

" first saw it about 12 or 13 years ago and I was astounded at its power. Basically the idea of doing a movie about Karen Carpenter using Barbie dolls is a deliciously, funny idea. The audience always cracks up for the first ten minutes but what's astounding about it is how much you start to identify with the dolls. So by the end of the film when she's dying you're in tears.

Part of its allure is that it is the most talked about unseen film. I've heard that there are video stores that if you use the right code word they'll give it to you. I know that there are bootleg copies that turn up on E-bay. We made a plea to the Carpenters, to Richard not long ago to see if he'd let us show the film and donate the profits to eating disorder charities. He said no. I don't like it when I see it being sold, because I don't think that's fair, however I feel that bootlegging it is the only way

the movie has a life. So we don't stand in the way of that. "

In an industry in which the term "independent filmmaking" is increasingly becoming an oxymoron, producer Christine Vachon from Killer Films has been the force behind some of the most exciting and original cinema to emerge from the US over the past decade. A long-time champion of maverick talents, Vachon's producer credits include Todd Solondz's *Happiness*, Mary Harron's *I Shot Andy Warhol*, the Oscar-winning *Boys Don't Cry* and three films by Todd Haynes: *Poison*, *Safe* and *Velvet Goldmine*. She also acted as co-producer on Larry Clark's *Kids*. Forthcoming projects include Solondz's latest picture, *Storytelling*, the acclaimed high-camp musical *Hedwig And The Angry Inch* and an adaptation of AM Holmes' collection of short stories, *The Safety Of Objects*, to be directed by another long-term collaborator, Rose Troche.

TEXT BY **WENDY IDE**

Ernesto Esposito

ANOTHER THING I Wanted To Tell You

by Noel Godin, Provocateur

Anthology Of Radical Subversion by Noel Godin and The Theory Of The Four Movements by Charles Fourier.

"My own book tells how to destroy a world that destroys us, while Charles Fourier's book explains that we can replace this abject world with a world where passion and reason combine in the most poetic, burlesque and libidinous manner, with the reign of pleasure everywhere. It's a world of crazy love, crazy humour and real intelligence, where everyone can realise their fantasies and all these things contribute to the social good.

If you don't retaliate against the powers that be, you're an accomplice to those in power. By throwing a simple cream pie, we take action against the powers that be. My friends from '68 - as well as young people I meet today - want to destroy everything in order to reconceive everything. That's why I believe in Charles Fourier. In the last three years, everything for me has started again. There's a utopian spirit which suffuses the current anti-globalisation struggle."

The Belgian "entarteur" anarchist Noel Godin has literally been firing pies in the face of the establishment for over 30 years. Conquests to date include the "greedy" Bill Gates, the "self indulgent" Jean-Luc Godard and the "pompous" French philosopher Bernard-Henri Lévy (five times veteran).

Godin's current plans include completing three books for publication this year, and improvising his part in Jan Bucquoy's controversial film *The Sexual Life Of The Belgians 5*. On his continued quest to find more dangerous, more damaging and more unexpected treats for the establishment, he has recently built a giant cream-pie Tartapulte with a trajectory of 35 metres. His intention? To pie the Pope himself. Each sentence in these books is packed with a rich subversive density and each line is a catastrophe for the establishment. They are a timeless call to arms against everything that prevents us from being ourselves.

NOEL GODIN PHOTOGRAPHED AT HOME IN BRUSSELS BY **BERT HOUBRECHTS** AND **KURT DE WIT**. TEXT BY **EMMA E FORREST**

ETRO

14 OLD BOND STREET, LONDON W1 – TEL. 0207 – 4955767

PH.: MICHAEL WOOLLEY

WOMEN'S COLLECTION AVAILABLE AT: BROWNS – HARVEY NICHOLS – LIBERTY
MEN'S COLLECTION AVAILABLE AT: SELFRIDGES – HARVEY NICHOLS – THE DUFFER OF ST. GEORGE – BROWN THOMAS, DUBLIN

ANOTHER THING I Wanted To Tell You
by Chan Marshall, Musician

Everything without a man-made imprint.

"It could be dark wet soil. It could be water in a vacant swimming pool, just the water, its reflection, its clarity. We're all moving and growing differently, as perfectly misplaced as everything in nature. To me, man-made things offer only a one-sided guarantee, superficial, supported, disconnected. Nature is a direct hit of all senses, your state of mind, your sense of freedom, and time." Atlanta-born Cat Power, otherwise known as Chan Marshall, is the unpredictable part punk, part hippie-mystic who took up the guitar in

'91 and hasn't stopped moving since. The bright star of what was once called the indie scene, Power had a vision on a trip to South Africa in '97 involving the appearance of a white Victorian vest she had seen in a dream. On her return to the US, she abandoned New York and moved into an old house in the rural South. There, she had a nightmare in which the devil tried to lure her into a field. From her spare, raw albums *What Would the Community Think?*, *Moon Pix*, *Myra Lee*, *Dear Sir* and last year's collection of covers, Cat Power has built a loyal following.

CHAN MARSHALL WAS PHOTOGRAPHED IN CENTRAL PARK BY **MARK BORTHWICK**. TEXT BY **EDWARD HELMORE**

Guseppe

GIUSEPPE ZANOTTI DESIGN

ANOTHER THING I Wanted To Tell You
by Hal Wilner, Music Producer

Ernie Kovacs, the innovative 50s American TV comedian.

"Ernie Kovacs seems to be virtually unknown outside America, and even there he's no longer a household name. He was an innovator and one of the great genius artists at a time when TV was still relatively young. Beyond just being an intellectual comic able to do almost anything, he was a great actor, a pioneer of television, an improviser of talk and variety shows, and a supreme surrealist. On TV in the '50s, he'd do video vignettes of apes dancing ballet to Swan Lake, people eating spaghetti to Stravinsky, and kitchens coming to life choreographed to Prokofiev. He thought up strange recurring characters such as Wolfgang von Sauerbrauten, German disk jockey, "schpinning der dischks"; Miklos Molnar, irascible Hungarian chef; Motzah Hepplewhite, drunken magician; Percy Dovetonsils, poet and Martini lover. Kovacs wasn't subversive in the political sense except that he wasn't politically correct and did everything with amazing sophistication. No one has ever bettered him."

Hal Wilner is an esteemed producer best known for his work with Lou Reed, Marianne Faithfull, William Burroughs and Allen Ginsberg. He famously produced tribute records to Charlie Mingus "Weird Nightmare", Kurt Weill "Lost In The Stars" and Edgar Allan Poe "Closed On Account Of Rabies" as well as the soundtracks for Robert Altman's *Shortcuts* and *Kansas City*, Gus Van Sant's *Finding Forrester* and Wim Wenders' *The Million Dollar Hotel*. Last year, Wilner organised a benefit concert featuring Nick Cave, Van Dyke Parks and David Johansen in aid of the archive of Harry Smith and the Anthology of American Folk Music.

ARCHIVE PHOTOGRAPH OF ERNIE KOVACS COURTESY OF EDIE ADAMS. TEXT BY **EDWARD HELMORE**

BE MATERIALISTIC

Pringle
SCOTLAND

ANOTHER THING I Wanted To Tell You
by Roman Coppola, Filmmaker

The futuristic designs of Professor Luigi Colani.

"I was doing some research in this bookstore in Santa Monica and I described to the book dealer this late '60s, early '70s, futuristic design that I was interested in. I had never seen Luigi Colani's work before and the dealer pulls out two sets of his books. It was exactly what I was looking for. Colani's style is really sensual and sexy. There's definitely something about the avant-garde culture of the '70s that I connect with strongly, probably because I was a teenager at that time. There are some direct references to his design in *CQ*; a scene near the end where the Billy Zane character comes down on his parachute and lands on the Eiffel Tower. He's in these Colani-designed full body helmets that look like ski jumper's helmets. He also designed motorcycles that are shaped like a body with two wheels. When I first discovered Colani I became quite obsessive. I got a Colani Pelikan pen and a computer mouse which I bought on eBay for $12, but which I can't use. It doesn't fit on my keyboard and ultimately it's just a weird pod-shaped mouse. It was funny to buy this totally useless lump of plastic that just looks cool."

Roman Coppola's debut feature film *CQ,* for which he also wrote the screenplay, is released in the US in October. Set to the backdrop of the May '68 riots in Paris, *CQ*, a dark comedy, is the story of a young filmmaker's conflict between making his own existentialist film and working on an out-of-control sci-fi, B-movie. It is a closely observed homage to the pscho-drama of filmmaking. Superbly shot and acted, *CQ* features Jeremy Davies, Angela Lindvall and Elodie Bouchez alongside Gerard Depardieu, Billy Zane and Jason Schwartzman. Roman Coppola has directed a string of critically acclaimed pop promos, most notably winning the MTV Music Video Awards with Spike Jonze for Fat Boy Slim's "Praise You". He has worked with the likes of Moby, Mansun, Air, Daft Punk and French electronic artists Mellow who scored the music for *CQ*.
FOR FURTHER INFORMATION ON LUIGI COLANI VISIT **WWW.COLANI.CH**

ROMAN COPPOLA AND A COLANI HELICOPTER. TEXT BY **JEFFERSON HACK**

ANOTHER THING I Wanted To Tell You

by Kim Gordon, Musician

Judee Sill, the haunting beauty of a 60s singer/songwriter.

"My friend Jim O'Rourke is always turning me on to different female vocalists, all of them I have loved. They seem to have an air of darkness, melancholy and unholy beauty. The last especially describes the music of Judee Sill, my current obsession. Her debut was actually the first album to be released on Asylum Records. That to me is weird. The whole time I was pining away as an angst-ridden teen girl listening to Joni Mitchell when I could have been grooving to Judee. It's a reminder of the workings or not, of major labels. One singer is promoted and the other one is left for future rediscovery oblivion. Judee's pop sense is incredibly sophisticated and her voice is totally soulful. My favorite songs are on the first record, "The Lamb Ran Away" and "Jesus Was A Crossmaker". I'm not sure how she died but she was pretty young and I miss her."

During punk rock's initial assault on the American consciousness, Kim Gordon was studying visual art in her native California. After graduating she moved to New York, where she worked on installation pieces and wrote for *artforum* magazine. It was in NYC that she met Thurston Moore and started playing an experimental hybrid of punk, jazz and modern composition. In '81 guitarists Moore and Lee Ronaldo formed Sonic Youth, with Gordon on bass. The band's output and influence has spanned the last 20 years - starting with *Confusion Is Sex* ('83) and culminating in last year's Nyc *Ghosts & Flowers*. During this time Gordon released a clothing line, *X-Girl*, produced Hole's first album, *Pretty On The Inside*, and toured the world.

KIM GORDON PHOTOGRAPHED BY **PIERRE BAILLY** IN HIS PARIS APARTMENT. TEXT BY **ROB MORGAN**

Zinco

ANOTHER THING I Wanted To Tell You
by Bruce Mau, Designer

"I have an interest in the literary capacity of the image and *Nothing Personal* is a model that hits the top note. Ostensibly a book about race in America in the early '60s, it is also an incredibly powerful collection of images combined with visually literate text. It is a kind of 'literature of America' that plays in two modes, a text and an image essay. James Baldwin completed the text; an essay about the separation between rhetoric and reality in America. Avedon then completed a set of images picturing that rhetoric. Working together, they both expose the reality of modern America by weaving in and out of each other so that you begin to read images in the same way that you read text. It is an incredibly powerful piece of work and points to different ways in which we are able to view the world around us."

Canadian Bruce Mau is a multi-disciplined designer in full-throttle. Since founding his Toronto-based studio in '85 he has maintained long-standing relationships with architects Frank Gehry and Rem Koolhaas (with whom he designed and conceived the book *S, M, L, XL* over five years) as well as producing installation work for many international institutions, from the Getty Research Institute to the Bilbao Guggenheim. Although committed to broadening the role of the designer, Mau is most well-known for his books and his concern with the relationship between image, text and page. Last year, he published the 640 page *Life Style*, a collection of essays, criticism and images questioning and discussing the importance of the surface in our lives.

NOTHING PERSONAL PHOTOGRAPHED BY **MATT HOLYOAK** AT SIMON FINCH RARE BOOKS LONDON (WWW.SIMONFINCH.COM). TEXT BY **DAVE CALHOUN**

JIGSAW

ANOTHER THING I Wanted To Tell You

by Benedikt Taschen, Publisher

Billy Wilder, the director of Some Like It Hot, Seven Year Itch and Stalag 17.

" Billy Wilder once said, 'As a director you don't have to be able to write, but it helps if you can read.' For me, being a publisher is similar; I can read quite well but I can hardly write. Therefore I'll borrow this wonderful quote which sums up Billy Wilder's gift, 'He has those rarest of human attributes, eyes and ears which look and hear with freshness, looking upon all things as if he is seeing them for the first time, looking with the eyes of a child and hearing with the ears of a musician who can hear melodies not heard by everyone. He has the sensitivities of a musician and a painter.' Variety is the spice of life and Wilder's films prove it. He has explored every genre, from film noir to comedy to romance and just about everything in between. As he says, 'I am not a comedy director. I am not a serious picture director. I am a director.' I would add that he is the director's director. Thank you, Billy Wilder."

German publisher Benedikt Taschen has been in the book business for over 20 years now. In 1980, he opened the tiny Taschen Comics Shop in Cologne selling new and rare collectors' comics, and started publishing his own comics a few years later. From these humble beginnings, Taschen has become a publisher of high quality art and photography books of world renown, producing collections for both the fully established, such as Leni Reifenstahl and Helmut Newton, and for those breaking through, like Wolfgang Tillmans and Natacha Merritt. In tribute to the great director, Taschen is publishing *Some Like It Hot - A Guide to The Billy Wilder Film* this autumn.

BENEDIKT TASCHEN PHOTOGRAPHED IN COLOGNE BY **OLIVER HELBIG**. TEXT BY **DAVE CALHOUN**

JIGSAW

ANOTHER THING I Wanted To Tell You
by Chris Ofili, Artist

UK soul trio Spacek's debut album, Curvatia.

"The thing I enjoy about hip hop is that it constantly reinvents itself. When I first heard Spacek at a Blueprint session in London, it just felt like new music to me. Yet it also had a degree of familiarity, with a soft emphasis on the beats which don't dominate the vocals. It's the kind of thing that grabs you. It grabbed me and compelled me to listen more. While I paint, it gently puts my mind off my work. It does this thing where you hear sounds through interruptions and the beat; but these sounds seem to disappear before you hear them. Before your brain registers them, they are gone. It's this feeling, along with a sense of generosity and intimacy, that makes you slow down your ear. This appeals to my current feeling of trying to keep things inside. It's a homely, warm feeling."

Since winning the Turner Prize in '98, British artist Chris Ofili continues to capture the attention of the art world, creating technically diverse work, layered with cultural references, inventiveness and humour. His most controversial work, *The Virgin Mary*, featuring a black Madonna with elephant dung on one breast set against a background of genitalia cut-outs caused a media scandle as part of the '99 Saatchi "Sensation" exhibition at the Brooklyn Museum of Art. Ofili's work can be seen in permanent collections at the Victoria & Albert Museum and Tate Gallery in London and the Museum of Modern Art in Manhattan.

CHRIS OFILI CIRCA 2000 IN A TREE SOMEWHERE CLOSE TO PARADISE. STILL LIFE SHOT BY **THOMAS C CARD**. TEXT BY **KATE EMELIANOVA**

JIGSAW

THE HUBBLE SPACE TELESCOPE, SITUATED 380 MILES ABOVE EARTH, HAS FOR OVER TEN YEARS CAPTURED THE MOST STUNNING IMAGES FROM DEEP SPACE.

SPACE - THE FINAL FRONTIER

TEXT **MARK SANDERS**

The history of astronomy is an ever-repeating cycle of expanding horizons and technological advancement. From Galileo's first telescope, which improved on the naked eye vision of the universe, to the complex assemblages of optics and electronics that we use today, astronomical discovery has risen - and fallen - on the strengths of the equipment used to achieve it. This is certainly true of the Hubble Space Telescope, named after the astrologer Edwin Hubble who first discovered the evolution and expansion of the galaxies in the 1920s. The first three years of scientific research into the formation of the universe was dogged by technical problems discovered after its launch into the earth's orbit in April 1990. After a spectacular space shuttle mission by NASA in December 1993 to implement corrective optics to the telescope's disabled mirror, Hubble was deemed fully operational and the first dramatic images of deep space were transmitted

A BUTTERFLY PLANETARY NEBULA (M29)

At a distance of 2,100 light years from Earth and situated in the constellation Ophiuchus in the Milky Way galaxy, the butterfly planetary nebula is a bi-polar nebula of two stars in perilously close orbit, emitting twin exhausts of gas at speeds in excess of 300 kilometres per second. This velocity places the origin of the stellar outburst at just 1,200 years ago.

THE SUN

An ordinary G2 star, one of billions in the Milky Way galaxy and the central star of our solar system. Spherical and gaseous with an equatorial diameter of 1,306,000km, energy is produced at its core by the nuclear fusion of hydrogen into helium, a process that will cease in about five billion years when cataclysmic death throes will ensue.

JUPITER

Mostly hydrogen, with small amounts of helium, ammonia, methane and water vapour. Adorned by distinctive light zones and dark belts, five or six in each hemi-sphere, which correlate to wind currents. Beset by violent storms, the largest and most persistent of which is the clearly visible Great Red Spot, itself the size of Earth. Wind speeds can reach 530km per hour.

MERCURY

Never further then 28 degrees from the Sun, Mercury has almost no atmosphere and is subject to massive temperature fluctuations - from 700K to 100K at night, with a mean of 440K. The surface is heavily cratered, not dissimilar to that of the Moon, with the largest impact scar, the Caloris Basin, having a diameter of 1300kms.

back to the Space Telescope Science Institute on earth. Today, over 400 observation programs are scheduled each year and have helped to create a unique picture of the planets, our solar system and the past evolution of the universe.

Some of the telescope's most impressive images have been courtesy of its Faint Object Spectrograph and the Hubble Deep Field program which allow astronomers to probe the hidden secrets of the cosmos, calculated to be around 12 billion years old. Gazing serenely at galaxies that were born only a few billion years after the Big Bang, Hubble's unique advantage over ground based observatories is that it is able to focus light without hindrance from the Earth's atmosphere. In a single patch of sky in the region of Ursa Major, Hubble has identified nearly 3,000 galaxies each containing thousands of individual stars and solar systems. Hubble has even allowed astrologers

VENUS

Often dubbed the "morning/evening star", Venus rotates slowly in a retrograde direction to Earth. Atmosphere is 96 per cent carbon dioxide, four per cent nitrogen with traces of water vapour, oxygen, neon, argon, sulphur dioxide and sulphuric acid. The surface, permanently obscured by dense clouds of dilute sulphuric acid, has a surface pressure 90 times that of the earth and a mean temperature of 730K.

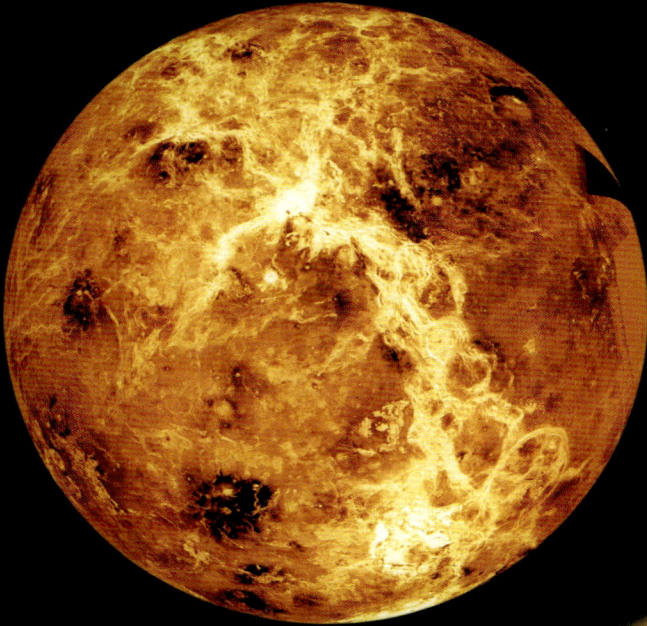

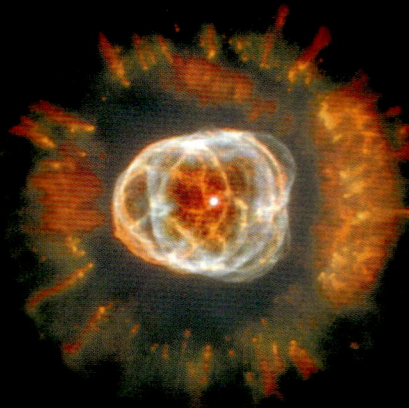

THE ESKIMO NEBULA (NGC2392)

At a distance of 5,000 light years from earth in the Gemini constellation in the Milky Way, the Eskimo Nebula is the luminous remnants of a dying star not unlike our own Sun. The bright central region is a series of elongated bubbles of debris, each about one light year long, being blown into space at speeds of up to 0.5 million kilometres per hour.

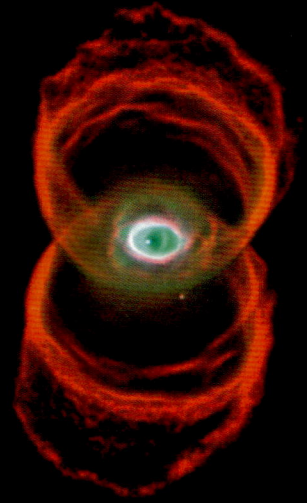

THE HOURGLASS NEBULA (MYCN18)

At a distance of 8,000 light years from Earth, the Hourglass Nebula forms part of the Milky Way. Its hourglass shape is produced by the surge of a fast stellar wind within a slowly expanding cloud, more dense near its equator than at its poles. Ionised nitrogen is shown in red, hydrogen in green and double-ionised oxygen in blue.

MARS

Atmosphere predominately carbon dioxide with traces of nitrogen, argon and oxygen, the surface itself is cratered and pitted and includes an immense system of canyons. The Valles Marineris is 5,000kms in length, and the extinct volcano, Olympus Mons, 26kms in height and 550kms in diameter. Dried-up flow channels that scar much of the surface indicate that Mars once saw the existence of large quantities of water and possibly life.

> to formulate a pattern for the life and death of stars, from star birth, in which the young star is born through nuclear fusion between hydrogen and helium, to star death and the dramatic formation of white dwarfs and black holes. It is calculated that the average life of a star is around 10 billion years with the Sun being approximately half way through its life cycle.

Closer to home, both the Hubble Space Telescope and other more conventional space satellites have contributed to our understanding of the make-up and composition of the planets. Probing the different atmospheric conditions on Mars and Jupiter, Venus, Saturn and the icy expanse of Pluto, they have become our eyes and ears in space, providing a glimpse of the lives of planets and distant galaxies expanding billions of years back in time to the moment when the universe first came into being.

ALL IMAGES COURTESY OF NASA AND BLUESPACE. FOR FURTHER INFORMATION AND IMAGES OF THE COSMOS FROM THE HUBBLE SPACE TELESCOPE AND OTHER CONVENTIONAL SPACE SATELLITES PLEASE CONTACT THE BLUE GALLERY AT BLUEGALLERY@COMPUSERVE.COM. HUBBLE VISION: FURTHER ADVENTURES WITH THE HUBBLE SPACE TELESCOPE, IS PUBLISHED BY THE UNIVERSITY OF CAMBRIDGE PRESS PRICED £25. ENQUIRIES +44 1223 312 393 OR WWW.CUP.ORG

ANOTHER THING I Wanted To Tell You
by Simon Doonan, Creative Director

Plexiglas portrait of George Clinton by Steve Caliguiri.

" This portrait is probably one of the most over-the-top, grotesque, and yet fabulous things that I've ever seen. To me, it's a constant reminder of the utter pointlessness of good taste. It is also very inspirational to me because it manifests the importance of fun and humour in art. People look at it and they smile. Actually, all Steve's work is brilliant and very amusing, including his portraits of Asian porno queens in the Co-op area at Barney's Uptown, and of budgies at Barney's in Chelsea. He is the King of Plexi, and his work is a bold celebration of fun and bravado, without any of the heavy pomposity of so much art today. I think there is a profundity in the fact that art can be hilarious. "

Simon Doonan is best known as Creative Director of the fashion temple, Barney's, NY. He is also a columnist for the *New York Observer.* As a creative impresario, Simon is responsible for all aspects of Barney's innovative, often controversial, but always entertaining, window displays and overall store image. Involved in the cutting-edge of fashion and pop culture for over 20 years, he has collaborated with Armani, Lagerfeld, Lacroix, as well as Rauschenberg, La Chapelle and Mapplethorpe. His hilarious autobiography, *Confessions Of A Window Dresser*, was published to much acclaim in '98 and is now in production through Maverick Films and New Line Cinema.

CONFESSIONS OF A WINDOW DRESSER IS PUBLISHED BY PENGUIN STUDIO.

SIMON DOONAN PHOTOGRAPHED BY **MARCELO KRASILCIC** IN HIS NEW YORK APARTMENT. TEXT BY **KATE EMELIANOVA**

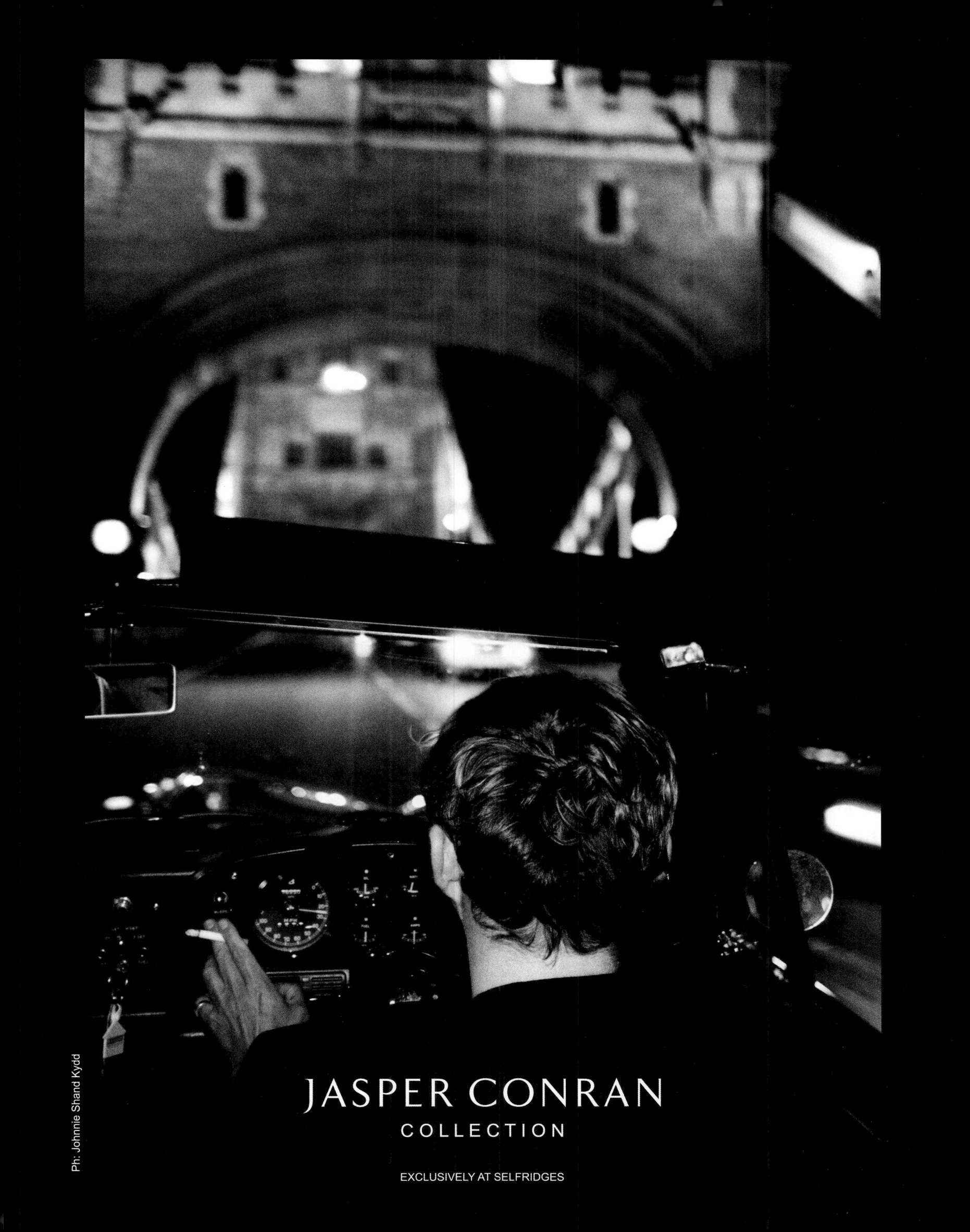

JASPER CONRAN

COLLECTION

EXCLUSIVELY AT SELFRIDGES

ANOTHER THING I Wanted To Tell You
by Terry Gilliam, Filmmaker

My own sketchbook, to remind me of who I was and what I have become.

"Everybody should keep their own sketchbook or diary and cling to it dearly. It's the only way you will know some years later what the world was, whether you've changed or not and how much you've been seduced and corrupted by everything around you. I was watching all these nostalgic television programmes recently about the '80s and they were making me more and more crazy because I began to accept their version of my past. What bothered me was that my past was being taken away from me. Trying to hold on to your own individuality, your own view of the world, is the most important thing you can do. I started looking back at my sketchbooks, the notes I'd written and ideas I'd had and I realised that during these periods I had a different view of the world. I want people to record their individual view of things. You can then go back to it and you might actually discover it's not your view at all. You thought it was your view, but it had been manipulated totally."

It all began with a big cartoon foot. Animator, designer and filmmaker Terry Gilliam moved to England from America in the late '60s and soon became the resident cartoonist for *Monty Python's Flying Circus*, going on to either co-direct or design on all the wonderfully bizarre Python films, *Monty Python* and the *Holy Grail*, *The Life Of Brian* and *The Meaning Of Life*. He has been making his own films since '77, including *Jabberwocky*, *Brazil*, *The Fisher King* and, most recently, *Fear And Loathing In Las Vegas*. Colourful, funny and weird, Gilliam's world is very much his own.

TERRY GILLIAM PHOTOGRAPHED IN LONDON BY **WILLIAM SELDEN**. TEXT BY **DAVE CALHOUN**

DAKS
LONDON E1

0800 288188 www.daks.com

ANOTHER THING I Wanted To Tell You
by Karyn Kusama, Filmmaker

Russian filmmaker Elem Klimov's 1985 film, Come And See.

"First of all, this film about the 1943 German invasion of the Soviet Union has been little seen and it really is such a great film. It follows a young child and failed partisan, Florya, and when I saw it first what struck me was that it had the guts to be poetic, to be a lyrical film, despite its context of war. That was a bold choice, not to prettify it at all and to enoble absolutely no one. It's a stark portrait of humanity and our human shortcomings. I appreciated its confident, complete feeling. It felt like a psychologically complete movie."

Karyn Kusama's debut movie, *Girlfight,* depicted a hot-headed Brooklyn teenager as she realised her ambition to become a boxer. The film won Kusama a directing award at Sundance and she is now working on her follow-up, a sci-fi movie.

KARYN KUSAMA PHOTOGRAPHED BY **VANINA SORRENTI** AT HER BROOKLYN APARTMENT. TEXT BY **DAVE CALHOUN**

VIA SPIGA

WHEN ANIMALS ACQUIRE THE POWER OF HUMAN
COMMUNICATION, TO WHAT LENGTHS CAN WE GO TO
SATISFY THEIR DESIRES?

LANGUAGE IS POWER

PHOTOGRAPHY ALEXEI HAY
TEXT ALISON POWELL

"DID YOU BRING THE CAR? I WANT TO GO FOR A RIDE." Dr Lyn Miles, a professor of anthropology at the University of Tennessee, Chattanooga, looks at her adoptive son, her face etched with regret. "No," she says, "I'm sorry. We can't take the car." His face falls, he tells her he's annoyed, and walks off to see what his friends are doing over on the swings. He walks... on his knuckles.

Chantek [pictured left] is a 23-year-old orangutan living at Zoo Atlanta, in Georgia. For much of his life though, he was raised as Dr Miles's "cross-foster son" and enjoyed the car rides, summer holidays, television, videos, and McDonald's Happy Meals that are the entitlement of any suburban American upbringing.

Today, he sits across from us in a zoo habitat, lush with bamboo and grass, separated from "mother Lyn" by a 15-foot concrete moat. They are joined, however, as they have been since he was one-year-old, by a common language of human culture and a vocabulary. His tally to date is some 2,000 words in American Sign Language. But this afternoon will not be a stellar performance of communication: he's disappointed about the car and, as any rebellious son would, he's gone into a sulk.

Chantek is the only orangutan in the world who can use sign language and, therefore, speak for himself. He is the first of a new subset, what Miles calls a "bridge between species". "When I ask him who he is. He says he is an ORANGUTAN-PERSON."

That apes possess formidable brain power and social savvy is nothing new. How many Tarzan movies and screwball comedies have traded easily on the mass acceptance of primate intelligence? What is ground-breaking in Atlanta is the sophistication with which they are now able to express this rich inner world. And while Chantek may be the only orangutan who chastises his keepers for bringing the wrong brand of mineral water, he is not the only ape in the neighbourhood to be taught to communicate with us.

The area is home to the Language Resource Center, which draws researchers to projects that hand chimpanzees and their quiz-show smart cousins, bonobos, the tools of culture and language. Georgia State University's A-list ape Panbashiba boasts a vocabulary of 3,000 words, spoken through a keyboard of symbols, and at the Living Links Center, Frans de Waal explores the cutting edge of evolutionary thought and how it relates to animal culture.

Gaining person status, it turns out, requires a slender but critical clutch of traits. There must exist intelligence and the ability for rational thought. (Chantek has the verbal skill of a two-year-old human child and the thought processes of an eight-year-old; anything over age seven is considered an age of reason.)

But, according to Miles, the crucial "key concept" to being considered a conscious, sensate creature is, "A sense of self, some kind of agency or control. He makes his emotions very clear and that gives him an advantage over the other animals."

These other, equally intelligent beings have to sit here in the field and wait for their food to arrive, while Chantek can say, "I'D LIKE CHEESEBURGERS WITH SECRET TOMATO PASTE." [ketchup] "Language," Miles adds, "is power."

Chantek knows about lipstick and invented a sign for contact lens solution, which he saw his trainers using. He knows what a jacket and hat are for: in the past if he got cold he'd put on a jacket with extra long arms. But these days the zoo puts him out without any kind of clothes. "The zoo is concerned about how the public might react to an orangutan wearing clothes," Miles explains.

Thanks to what is known in field work as "enculturation" - the exposure to human culture paired with a means of expression -

these apes may be finally living out their intellectual destiny, but they are also no longer the innocents they once were. As Miles sees it, "I have an ethical responsibility because I have created an animal that can bridge the gap between animal and human worlds.

It's not just that these apes have a biological similarity to us, but they are also deeply feeling creatures capable of symbolic thought." Sometimes that symbolic thought shows itself by asking for a cheeseburger, what Chantek calls "CHEESEMEATBREADS".

But just as often, he gives unsettling glimpses of thought and feeling we mistake as humanising. This is a creature whose native ground is the thick jungle of Borneo, yet he grew up in a bedroom with sheets he could hide under. He listened to stories before bed and often showed concern for the characters in the books: "DID THE DOG DIE?" or "WHERE'S THE BIRD?". He also used to have bad dreams and would tell "mom" about his mortal fear of cats.

But equipping Chantek, or any other animal, with the skills of communication presents a dilemma. Once we are presented with hard evidence that some animals are indeed cognitively advanced, what do we do with it? And more importantly, how do humans rationalise our spot as top dog, evolutionarily speaking? Chantek, for instance, is upset by the same things we are. If he is mistreated or lied to, he will become angry and says so. These apes know the signs for "cry", "hurt", and "sad", they know "sorry" and they know things can be "good" and "bad". In other words, they have a vocabulary of emotions and there is no going back. When asked how Chantek feels about his exceptional situation, Miles says, "I imagine it's lonely."

But that solitude will surely lessen as more and more animals are granted a spot in the intelligence community. This past May, two unrelated studies found that dolphins - already considered among the smartest and most complex non-humans - are able to recognise themselves in a mirror, something Miles says is another part of being a person, a sign of self-awareness, and something of which Chantek is capable. In fact, the bottlenose dolphin is the first non-primate to demonstrate this level of recognition. The new studies also indicate that they can differentiate between themselves, and in this case humans, as individuals.

The implications of the work Miles is doing with Chantek and the strides made by scientists at the Language Research Center are clearly far reaching. As it often does, knowledge creates a problem. Humans striving to set themselves apart from, and well above, the animal kingdom point to rational thought and emotion as the dividing line - a line in the process of being rubbed out. Once you give animals or animal-persons the means to express their wishes, how do you deny them? Miles acknowledges, "It's not realistic that Chantek, at 250 pounds, would wander freely in our society, but he could have some choices in a very limited range. Already Chantek is frustrated because he's not getting the things he asks for, like wrenches, screwdrivers, and the materials for his artwork. He paints and he made me this necklace." Her vision is a primate cultural centre where apes could, for example, indicate to the keepers their needs and desires.

Chantek looks at us soulfully from across the moat and Miles hurries to include him in our conversation: "Chantek, we're talking about the movie *Planet Of The Apes*. You saw that, remember? The orangutans were the teachers and the people lived the same as apes today." Chantek, still sulking over the denial of the quarter pounder and a spin down highway 75, cocks an orange eyebrow and replies, "CAN I HAVE AN APPLE?" ▌

Cesare Paciotti

11 OLD BOND STREET, LONDON

CESARE PACIOTTI
VIA SANT'ANDREA 8, MILANO

FOR THE MOST LITTLE ADDED TO THE MINUTE,
ARCHITECTURAL FIX, YOU ONLY NEED TO SLIP OUT
DOWN A DESIGNER STORE OR STREET IN ANY FASHION
CAPITAL OF THE WORLD.

INSPIRATION INSTALLATION

FOR THE MOST INTENSE AND UP-TO-THE MINUTE ARCHITECTURAL FIX, YOU ONLY NEED TO SAUNTER DOWN A DESIGNER-STOCKED STREET IN ANY FASHION CAPITAL OF THE WORLD.

INSPIRATION INSTALLATION

PHOTOGRAPHY **MATHIAS KESSLER**
TEXT **HELEN CASTLE**

In New York, where designer names dominate entire districts rather than small enclaves, the effect is amplified. Strung out along Madison Avenue alone are John Pawson's Calvin Klein, a mid '90s rendition of minimalism par excellence, Peter Marino's Emporio Armani and Daniel Rowen's Michael Kors, which combines the minimal with all the warmth of a boudoir. Antonio Citterio and Partners' restrained Cerrutti Shop and newly opened Ungaro boutique, like Rowen's shop for Kors, combine reductivism with a certain sophisticated domesticity - dark oriental hardwoods and chaise-longues. And around the corner from Madison on East 60th is Michael Gabellini's spare but sensuous Nicole Farhi. Downtown in SoHo where the clientele are sassier, hipper and more media-orientated, the competition among fashion retailers for innovative spaces is even fiercer. Richard Gluckman's '99 fashion store and more recent perfumery for Helmut Lang on Greene Street have yet to be beaten. Two pared-down shops, positioned on opposite sides of the street, they retain the authentic rawness of the warehouse district with dramatic ceiling heights, glazed concrete floors and plain white walls - all features that work seamlessly with the specially commissioned art installations. The most notable of these is Jenny Holzer's digital display of provocative text on the columns framing the cash desk. A block down on Wooster Street is Gluckman's Yves Saint Laurent, which features a dedicated art gallery at the front of the store. At the corner of Spring and Wooster stands the tiny Issey Miyake shop, Pleats Please, designed by Harvard professor Toshiko Mori, which lures people in with its misted glazed elevation, layered structure and the teasing brightness of its conspicuous pea-green changing room. Still on Wooster is the highly stylised Costume National, whose strong geometries are evocative of Fritz Lang's *Metropolis*. It is the work of SHoP, a young practice who are currently the talk of Manhattan, and the architects of the USA's first Museum of Sex, on Lower Fifth Avenue, which will be completed for the end of the year. It is, however, the prospect of Rem Koolhaas' much-publicised new shop for Prada, located on the ground floor of the Guggenheim

SoHo Building, that is catapulting fashion retail into an entirely new architectural realm.

Koolhaas' engagement by Prada epitomises fashion's current infatuation with architecture, for Koolhaas is one of the most celebrated architects in the world, at the most celebrated moment in his career. In '97, Koolhaas published his architectural blockbuster *S, M, L, XL* (which is rumoured to have sold 100,000 copies - no small feat for an architectural book costing £50); and in 2000, he was awarded the Pritzker Prize - the architectural equivalent of the Nobel. Since then he has received the profession's highest accolade, a commission to design a Guggenheim Museum. This places him alongside Frank Gehry and Frank Lloyd Wright.

The appointment of an architect of Koolhaas' stature to design retail space is a recent phenomenon. Up until now, Prada's ubiquitous chain of pink and mint green shops were all designed by a low-profile Italian architect, who was firstly a friend and long-term associate of the Prada family. Holly Brubach, the ex-fashion critic of *The New Yorker* and Style Editor of the *New York Times Magazine*, brought Koolhaas to Miuccia Prada and Patrizio Bertelli's attention, while she was the Director of Home Collections at Prada. (Since then she has set up Studio Holly Brubach - her own consultancy in Milan and New York - which advises fashion clients on their choice of architects). Koolhaas was one of the ten architects whose work she put forward for the Pradas to select. She sums up the situation as it appeared at the time, "It seemed to me that there were two directions Prada could take: either commission some world-famous architect whose position in his field would be comparable to Prada's in fashion, or to give some new young talent a break." What is clear is that by opting for Koolhaas, Prada, a premier league fashion house, were unable to resist all the associated kudos and glamour that a premier league architect could bring. Prada do not stand alone in this respect. You only have to look at the commissions of the current architectural crème de la crème - the Pritzker Prize winners of the last ten years - to realise just ➤

Prada by REM KOOLHAAS

Issey Miyake by STANTON WILLIAMS

Helmut Lang by RICHARD GLUCKMAN

> how prevalent a phenomenon it has become: Christian de Portzamparc ('94) is the designer of the most monumental edifice any fashion corporation has possibly ever built - the LVMH Tower in New York. Last Spring, Tadao Ando ('95) completed Giorgio Armani's Building in Milan to coincide with the collections. Renzo Piano ('98) is currently finishing the headquarters of the Japanese subsidary of the French group Hermès in Tokyo. Meanwhile, the winners of the last two years - Rem Koolhaas (2000) and Herzog and de Meuron ('99) - are both within the Prada fold. As well as the SoHo shop in New York, Koolhaas is designing flagship stores for Los Angeles and San Francisco - while Herzog and de Meuron are responsible for Prada's Production Centre in Terranuova, Italy, in addition to a Tokyo store. Prada's endorsement and confidence in Koolhaas does not, however, stop at architectural space. Over the last three years, he has also overseen a research project to determine Prada's global strategy and mastermind their web presence.

Of course, the hype surrounding the new Prada stores - a book was brought out about their development even before they are open - gives them a lot to live up to. Jan Kaplicky, the founding principal of Future Systems, remains sceptical about their success as physical spaces. Koolhaas is famous for his books and his ideas rather than his architectural details. The strength of shops, Kaplicky maintains, lies in their details. Jan's remarks are shored up by the fact that over the last two years Future Systems has led their own revolution in retail design. The shops they have produced for Comme de Garçons and Marni have turned shop design on its head, single-handedly lifting the shackles of mid '90s minimalism. Future Systems first raised a finger to the status quo in early '99 with the extraordinary space-age aluminium entrance tunnel that they created for the Comme de Garçons store in West Chelsea, New York. This beautiful and highly original structure, without ribs or supports, had an explosive impact. It was completely unique. After their entrance tunnel, Future Systems went on to produce two further different solutions for Comme de Garçons stores - a glass elevation for the Paris shop and a curved wall for the shop in Tokyo. It was, however, the Marni shop in Sloane Street, completed in the autumn of 2000, which really captured the public imagination. Its now familiar turquoise walls

and curvaceous chrome fittings were splashed across the pages of the fashion press as well as the broadsheets. Future Systems had in a single strike brought colour and creativity back into shop design. Modestly, Kaplicky attributes their success to the simple fact that every fashion house requires a different solution.

Kaplicky is not interested in replicating signature architecture for a portfolio of clients. To illustrate this, he draws an analogy between shops and catwalk models. From the choice of models at catwalk shows, it is apparent that each fashion house has their own individual take on physical beauty. Shops, as physical spaces displaying clothes, ought to capture this essential difference.

It is likely that before too long, the present love affair between established houses and signature architecture will vascillate; it could well turn into a gauge for discovering young talent. It is not too hard to imagine that the all-too-studied approach of Koolhaas at Prada for creating shops that are "destinations" could engender a new appetite for the truly gritty, spontaneous and authentic. Young designers, such as Joe Hunter and Adam Thorpe, at Vexed Generation, already have a strong following among design-literate clientele working in the film, design, media and public industries; both locally in London's Soho and over in the States. Their shops, however, have real content. Rather than being architect-designed they put them together themselves. Joe Hunter describes the shops as "year-long catwalk shows". Each individual shop's installation is conceived alongside a collection, dispensing with the expense of "showing" to a small group of VIPs. The four installations they have created so far communicate larger ideas about civil justice, air pollution and surveillance. Dissent is also already apparent at the very heart of London's luxury shopping district - on the hallowed ground of Old Bond Street. Amid the beautiful sanctified spaces of DKNY, Prada and Gucci, with their doormen and haughty assistants, humour has been injected in the form of Camper. This Spanish footwear shop, designed by Marti Guixe, draws you in, tempting you to remove a shoe from one of its velcroed walls or sit on one of its big rubber balls. With its accessible playfulness, it eschews the high-minded aesthetics of its neighbours with their luxury marbles and woods. Only going to show that nothing, not even architecture, in this very fickle and ever changing world of fashion can be fixed ▮

HELEN CASTLE IS EDITOR OF ARCHITECTURAL DESIGN. THE FASHION AND ARCHITECTURE ISSUE IS AVAILABLE AT £19.99 FROM JOHN WILEY & SONS, ISBN 0471-49627-8, TEL (+44) 1243 843294.

A SHORTLIST OF ARCHITECTURAL PROJECTS TO LOOK OUT FOR:

PRADA:
SOHO, NEW YORK AUTUMN 2001 OMA/AMO REM KOOLHAAS
RODEO DRIVE, BEVERLEY HILLS LOS ANGELES AUTUMN 2002 OMA/AMO REM KOOLHAAS
SAN FRANSISCO SPRING 2003 OMA/AMO REM KOOLHAAS

ISSEY MIYAKE:
TRIBECA, NEW YORK AUTUMN 2001 FRANK GEHRY/ GORDON KIPPING

PAUL SMITH:
PARIS, SPRING 2002 SOPHIE HICKS ARCHITECTS

VEXED GENERATION:
SOHO, LONDON AUTUMN 2001

CALVIN KLEIN:
PARIS 2002 JOHN PAWSON

JIL SANDER:
LONDON SPRING 2002 GABELLINI ASSOCIATES
DUSSELDORF AUTUMN 2001 GABELLINI ASSOCIATES
RODEO DRIVE LOS ANGELES SUMMER 2002 GABELLINI ASSOCIATES
NEW YORK SUMMER 2002 GABELLINI ASSOCIATES

MARNI:
PARIS AUTUMN 2001 FUTURE SYSTEMS

SELFRIDGES:
BIRMINGHAM, ENGLAND 2003 FUTURE SYSTEMS

HARVEY NICHOLS:
BIRMINGHAM, ENGLAND AUTUMN 2001 FOUR IV

HELMUT LANG:
US AND EUROPE 2002 ONWARDS RICHARD GLUCKMAN

DOLCE & GABBANA:
MOSCOW SUMMER 2001 DAVID CHIPPERFIELD
NEW YORK WINTER 2001 DAVID CHIPPERFIELD
PARIS 2002 DAVID CHIPPERFIELD

ARMANI:
MILAN AUTUMN 2001 THEATRE AND EXHIBITION SPACE TADAO ANDO

Comme des Garçons entrance tunnel by FUTURE SYSTEMS

LOEWE

www.loewe.com
130, New Bond Street
Harrods, Room of Luxury
Selfridges Accessories Hall
LONDON

INSPIRATION | NICOLE FARHI

PHOTOGRAPHY HELMUT NEWTON AT MACONOCHIE PHOTOGRAPHY
INTERVIEW BRUCE ROBINSON
TEXT ROGER MORTON

YOU COME ALONG TO TURN ON EVERYONE

JUDE

YOU COME ALONG TO TURN ON EVERYONE

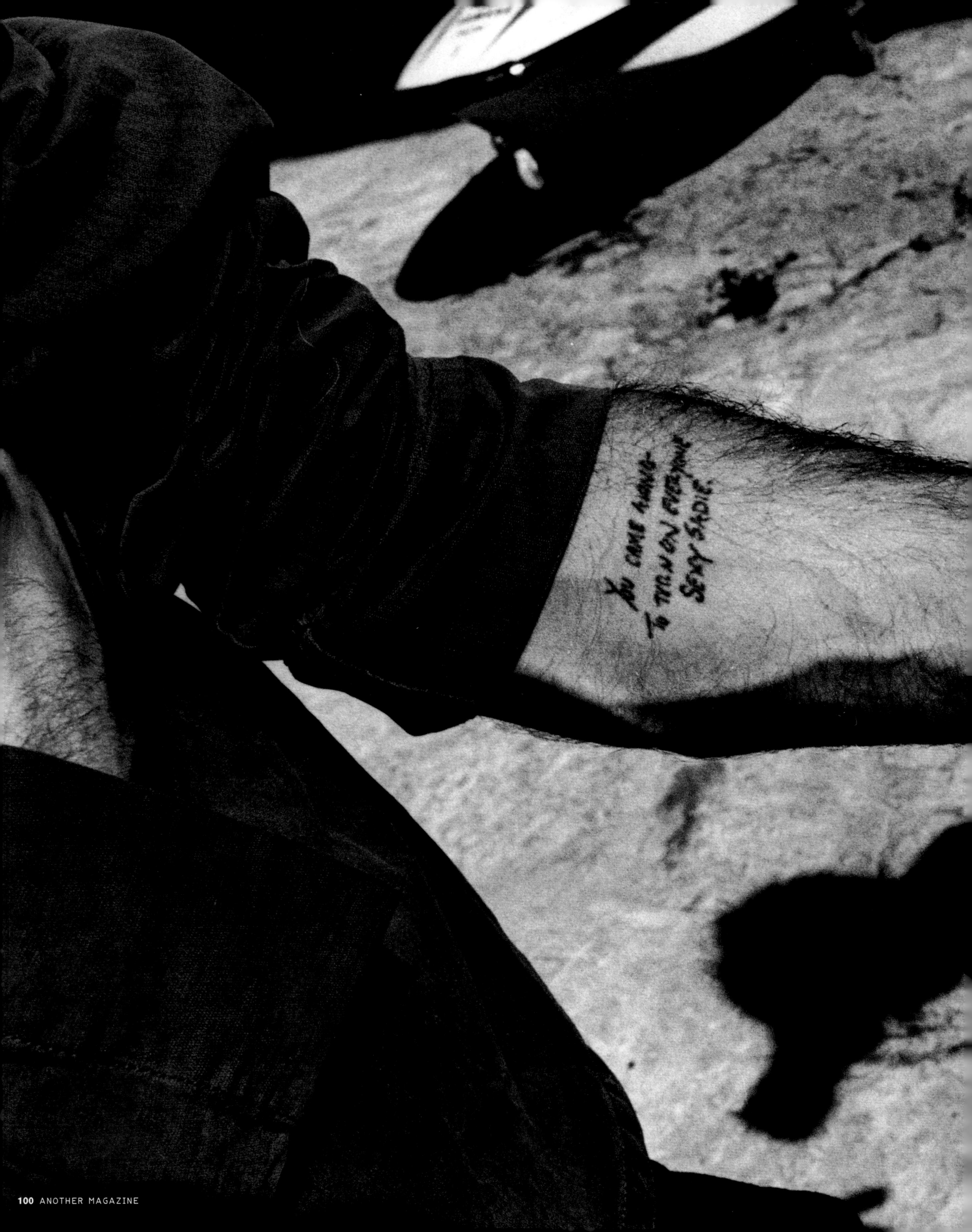

Jude Law has a theory about World War II. It takes into account the way his father eats chocolate, as if it's still rationed, and the way that George W Bush reacts to the Chinese, as if they're under the bed. He's come to the conclusion without really noticing it, that we're still living the Second World War. There are, maybe, two conclusions to be drawn from this cogitation on what came from where; that Jude Law is not just a pretty face and that history never lets go of the future.

If you further extend Law's law of infinite causality, it's because of the Beatles that he's in a North London pub, jawing about the Second World War and pub decor with the outspoken, inspirational writer/director Bruce Robinson.

It goes like this: Law was nudged down the path of destiny by the songwriting teamwork of Lennon and McCartney. His teacher parents named him after "Hey Jude" as well as Hardy's *Jude The Obscure*, which meant in the gang culture environment of his first school, Kidbrooke in Eltham, he was labelled a "poof" and picked on by the thug element.

At 14, Law's parents relocated their Brecht-loving teenager to a more theatrical-friendly private school, Alleyns in Dulwich. Jude got though his formative years without much of a class brand on him, and a natural born social chameleon actor was formed, with a blend of grace and grit that would eventually make him the most adored British star in generations.

In turn, Robinson was given a free hand to direct his script for *Withnail And I* thanks to the production involvement of George Harrison's Handmade Films. *Withnail And I* boomeranged Robinson into 14 more years of screen adventures, until he turned his attention to novels and hanging out down the pub with incandescent movie stars from Lewisham.

History won't let the future go. The War invented the '60s. The Beatles did it for Jude and in a way for Bruce, who made a rare acting appearance in '98, playing a guitarist from the '60s in *Still Crazy*. And Jude Law is married to actress Sadie Frost, daughter of David Vaughan, the '60s psychedelic pop artist who revolved in the art scene that grew up around The Beatles. Meanwhile Jude's still planning to play Brian Epstein, in a long-mooted biopic of the tragic manager's life.

Destined to meet then, probably with a little help from Hitler, or whoever rejected him from art school, and The Beatles, Jude and Bruce converge in a nostalgically quiet pub, the last jukebox free pub in London, to work their way towards the central issue of now as opposed to back then: the question of whether you can become something in the 2000s, without the entertainment industry and its marketing stormtroopers, and "info-tainment" dissemination thought police sapping the soul out of all that you work on, and everything you ever wanted to represent.

According to Bruce Robinson, the pivotal line in *Withnail And I* is when Danny the dealer says, "They're selling hippy wigs in Woolworths, man." Will they soon be selling Jude Law jumpers in Gap? In film promo interviews Law has consistently asserted his desire for integrity, his commitment to challenging, quality work and his distaste for celebrity. However, after the full-blown American stardom that *Mr Ripley* generated, prime LA hills real estate is his for the asking, and the Faustian banquet of fame, power and ego is laid out.

Prior to Ripley, Law observed that, "It's funny the way the pressures arrive, they come with silk gloves, you know." In which case the gloves are a lot closer to his throat this year.

This spring's release, *Enemy At The Gates,* saw him playing his straightest major part so far, as Stalingrad siege sniper Zaitsev, sinking in the dirt of the war machine. Close to £50 million was ventured on the questionable assumption that close ups of Law's eyes were mesmerising enough to carry you through an epic bloodbath. Some saw the role as a step onto the slippery silk path.

Law's full Hollywood beatification is, however, imminent, when he

plays a sex-god android in Steven Spielberg's *A.I. Artificial Intelligence*. Based on Brian Aldis' '69 short story, *Super Toys Last All Summer Long,* the cyber morality tale had been worked on for decades by Stanley Kubrick, who was planning to direct it after *Eyes Wide Shut*. Spielberg took over after Kubrick's death, casting child actor Hayley Joel Osment as the robo-kid looking for love and Law as Gigolo Joe, the ultimate, $100 million toy boy. From chatting with Spielberg about Kubrick on the future world set of *A.I.*, to down-the-pub with Robinson should be no stretch for Law. The normality of his London based family life with Sadie and the kids is something he's clung to fiercely; and there's more common ground between new darling Law and old warhorse Robinson than their Hollywood experiences. In Richard E Grant's film diaries, *With Nails,* Robinson is quoted as saying he was "as gorgeous as a fucking Renaissance Prince" when he left drama school, adding that various gents "wanted my arse". The writer's years as a "popstar pretty actor" mean he doesn't need to visit one of the many "Jude: The Adonis Of Our Times" - type web sites to appreciate Law's pin-up predicament.

As it transpires, however, even embodiments of Greek statuary with an affinity for Pre-Raphaelite lighting, scrub up mortal given the right company and a pint.

"I hate these things. The only reason I've turned this fucking thing on is because if I hadn't they'd have said 'You made it all up'," says Robinson, reluctantly setting the tape rolling. "I remember years ago when I did *The Killing Fields*, I went out to Thailand, and I was supposed to get into Cambodia but I was so freaked by the place I didn't make it. I'd never seen a dead body in my life until then. So I phoned John Swain from *The Sunday Times*. I said, 'Fucking [David] Puttnam's expecting me to turn up with all this "histoire de la guerre",' so John gave me a whole bunch of photographs from six years earlier and I took them to Puttnam and said, 'This is it David, this is where I was.'"

"I've never been to Cambodia, but I went to Vietnam about four years ago, which was a brilliant trip," enthuses Jude. "Actually it was our honeymoon, but even then you got a sense of danger. We wanted to spend two or three weeks there, so we were looking on the maps of where we could go, and we were near Laos and Cambodia, but we just chickened it. We thought, 'We've had such a good trip, we've tested a little bit of hot water. Maybe we won't jump right into it.'" "It's a pretty dangerous area," Robinson remarks. "If someone offs you on a jungle road what are you going to do? And then the next thing, the phone call's going through to Steven Spielberg. And Spielberg would be going, 'Jude's dead? OK. Well, what's Johnny Depp's number?'"

"I can just picture my dad searching for me," laughs Jude. "'I'm sure my son was here. He was on his honeymoon, he was definitely here at some point!'"

"I'm supposed to ask you about the new movie, *A.I.* How did you get on with Spielberg?"

"Great. It's one of those funny things. More than any other job, it was like a swanky car pulling up and someone saying, 'Get in.' You go on this amazing journey, and then they open the door and kick you out. But the journey and the car were great."

"I had a horrible fucking time with him [Spielberg], because I wrote a film essentially for him called *In Dreams*," recalls Robinson. "It ended up getting directed by Neil Jordan, an utter fucking disaster. It cost like $79 million and took about six at the box office. It was a fucking nightmare. I remember going out there and staying in this fucking shithouse hotel - always the same with billionaires isn't it? - put me in the cheapest fucking B&B. It was a non-smoking, non-drinking, Christian place on Long Island. It was when he was setting up his ranch."

"That is what is so spectacular, how he manages to juggle so much," interjects Jude. "He's so clever at fitting it into what he still has as his family life. We were rehearsing at his house while he was on holiday."

"I remember when I was at that hotel, the driver said, 'Do you mind meeting Steven on the boat this morning, he likes to be on the boat.' So I go down to the docks and there's all these heavies with earphones going, 'Mr Spielberg's arriving at the dock... Mr Spielberg's getting out of the car.' You can hear all of this because of the earphones. Then we get on the boat - I mean the guy's got a well upholstered post office account and the boat's from here to that door over there. We drive around the headland, and I'm thinking that *this* is the boat, until I see a fucking QE2 anchored there."

"And that was his boat?"

"Yeah, that was his boat! I liked him enormously, I must admit. He's probably a genius, but so is Mozart, and I don't like Mozart's music," says Bruce. "He somehow has a facility to tune his particular radio set into a 15-year-old mentality. A 15-year-old, highly intelligent mentality."

"I think also he even manages to bring out the 15-year-old in all of us, and even if you're 12 it makes you want to be 15," comments Jude. "What was interesting was the guy that I was playing did a lot of dancing and so I went and studied with a choreographer for three months. I mean Steven's a lot of things but he's not a dancer, and so it was quite interesting, suddenly me saying 'I wanna do this...' dooo dee doo dee dooo... over here, and him being like, 'Oh?... Well I'd better shoot it like this.' But it was cool, he adapted and we did that quite a lot, sort of breaking it down and him re-working it to shoot it as he wanted.

"I tell you what was interesting, the Kubrick presence," continues Jude. "He wasn't answering to him because he doesn't have to answer to anyone because of his track record, but he was sort of doing it *as him* if you like. There was a certain reverence, a spell to the whole thing that affected it and altered it in a way. I mean I've not worked with Kubrick before or even met him, but I imagine that it affected it. The secrecy around the piece was quite nice, there was no big bravado about it, no visitors or trips."

"I found an astonishingly benevolent selfishness about him," says Bruce. "Very friendly selfishness. But I wouldn't like to be up the wrong alley with him."

"I don't think you'd even know about it, I think he's one of those people where the coolness would come," says Jude.

"You'd be leaning over the gate going 'I am having lunch with him you know!'" (Bruce adopts strident American accent) "'YOU'RE NAAAT!' And it would take six people to get back to him, to know that you were looking over the gate."

Trying to get the attention of stellar directors is no longer a problem for Jude or his agent. 200 million people saw him outshine Matt Damon in *The Talented Mr Ripley*. BAFTA-awarded and Oscar-nominated as Best Supporting Actor, he's made it to the heart of brightness. Inevitably, however, there's now a question mark over whether Law can steer a healthy career path through the dazzle, whilst preventing the bleaching out of his daily private life.

No other successful British actor from recent times has lent themselves so perfectly to reductive celebritisation. Already listed in *People* magazine's Top 50 Most Beautiful People, Law gave in the region of 400 interviews for *Ripley*, most of them festishising his appearance, while the actor fought back with assertions of his boring, family-loving normality.

There's surreal comedy to be found in the porno-iconic dismembering of Jude - the "dashing", "devastatingly handsome", "Narcissus of British Cinema", with the "storm-dark eyes". Or are they "penetrating grey-green eyes", or even "blue-green eyes,

reckless with lashes"? But even if Law finds it funny, it's the kind of stuff that mounts up around a bloke from Lewisham, and leaves him suspicious of his own reflection.

Law doesn't read his press. Stoically, relentlessly, he tells the Adonis lobby that "anything that boxes you in as an actor is a pain in the arse". Yet it has to be disorientating to have directors casting you because of your "cat-like" eyes (Jean-Jacques Annaud, *Enemy At The Gates*) or discussing the way that your face "accepts light in such an interesting way" (Anthony Minghella after *Ripley*). Neither Oldman, Fiennes, Roth or even Ewan McGregor were faced with a full-blown DiCaprio syndrome.

No doubt, as a teen actor on poor Mancunian soap operas, Law had dreams of red carpets in California. The mid '90s "up and coming" phase of forming the Brit Pack production company Natural Nylon, and waiting for lfeboat roles in *Wilde* and *eXistenZ* (after a false start with *Shopping*) were surely marked by reveries of De Niro on the cellular. But as he discusses with Robinson - a former Oscar nominee himself for his script for *The Killing Fields* - having the gods grant your wishes brings a dissonant reality.

"There's this kind of merry-go-round, roller-coaster kind of pulp that comes with it all and I have to say, I've had it up to here with that really," says Jude. "I mean something like this, me and you, is a pleasure to me because I've wanted to meet you and I've read your stuff. But normally you're sitting with a fucking journalist, it's like, what is the pleasure in that? You feel like an arsehole because you're talking about yourself - you feel always a little bit like you're going to be caught out. I mean, you should want to talk about the work you've done, but it never really comes down to that and that, to me, is almost outweighing the enjoyment of work. And then the more work you do, the more you feel like you're not just being judged on 'oh that's quite an interesting job' or 'he took an interesting decision there with that part' or 'I wonder why he took that part?'. It's nothing to do with that anymore. It's always, 'Who does he think he is?', 'Who is he trying to fool?'"

"Yeah but you don't seem to work like that, you go back to the stage and do plays," counters Robinson. "This industry is about power, and fame is power, and if you haven't got power you're fucked."

"Yeah, but the purity and simplicity of writing a novel, for you, or doing a play, for me, to me nowadays absolutely outweighs..." Jude searches for clarity. "I mean, I still get excited if it's a great script and part, and someone says this guy's directing it, I think 'wow', but the more you do it, the more you remember that it's really going to be sitting around for five months, living in some weird bed and breakfast and I probably won't see my kids for two of those months and it will be a good part, but then I'll have to go on a press junket, and do... and do I really want to do that? I don't know."

"You have to," says Robinson.

"Yeah I suppose you have to," accepts Jude.

"One of the things that I can't dig about the cinema now is it's like building an aeroplane," continues Robinson. "You carry the most passengers, the furthest and the cheapest for the biggest profit, and I can't hack it. Like I've written this comedy and Rachel Weisz wants to do it, and I'd love to make it with her, but unless I can get Spielbergian control, I don't want to do it."

"Because you know the amount of time you'll have having arguments and fights," agrees Jude. "Maybe that's what I'm starting to realise, maybe that's the circle. You start out not quite knowing what you want to do, but you know that you want to get your foot in, and get involved with interesting, creative people. Then all of a sudden you're there, and somebody's giving you money for it and it's all going quite well. Then you suddenly think, 'Why do I want to do this?' and you don't think about it for a while and ›

> keep going. Then you realise, 'Actually, yeah, I don't want to bash my head around anymore, actually this isn't the journey I want to go on, I want to go back and do that now.'"

"Yeah, which I think is right and legitimate," says Robinson. "You get star vehicles, which are fantastic and it's great to be famous and make a load of dough, because fame, dough and ego are the currencies of the industry. If you've got fame and dough you can do what you fucking want, and that's what you need in this business. I have neither of those commodities, I'm sort of like an underground sniffer."

"But don't you realise you do have a commodity that probably 95 per cent of those people with fame and money want, which is respect and status?" points out Jude. "Respect is the one thing that people, really in the end, can't buy, can't barter for."

"I guess you can't," accepts Bruce. "But the only respect comes from me shuffling up this fucking street 38 years ago, going out drinking down The Engineer."

Robinson and Law pause to consider their surroundings, a modern "gastropub" which they decide compares unfavourably to old fashioned hostelries. To Jude's chagrin, even the nearby "proper old pub" favoured by the actor and his London friends, has been modernised. The semi-legendary Engineer, immortalised in *Withnail And I*, has gone up-market too. Naturally Jude is curious about Robinson's mid '60s memories of drinking in The Engineer with Vivian MacKerrel, the impoverished actor friend who provided the model for the flailing but spirited Withnail.

"The Engineer used to be the ropiest pub in North London," recalls Robinson. "The last time I ever had a drink with Vivian MacKerrel was in there. He drank himself to death, in the sense that he used to drink malt whiskey, and whiskey is a carcinogenic. He got cancer of the throat, he couldn't swallow or talk. He had a fucking pink tube coming out of his stomach with a funnel and a bottle of Lagavoulin going straight into his gut.

"The biggest coward and the bravest bastard I've ever met, because he laughed right up to the fucking end. I said to him, 'Christ, what about death?' and he said, 'It's nothing, it's a piece of piss.' The weird thing is that now *Esquire* magazine are doing a feature on the cunt. I mean, ha ha, he must be looking over the gates of Heaven."

"Yeah, I talk about this with Sadie quite a lot," ponders Jude. "About what's going to be interesting is how, as you said, this 'plastic-wrapped' generation of actors and popstars, artists, writers, all of us, when the tragedies and the real, almost Dickensian decay affects us, when we all get to a point where a few of us are dropping off. I mean it will be very interesting to see how and why and where that comes from, whether it's gonna be anorexia or bulimia or who will turn into the 60 pounds of... It will just be very interesting to see how it affects us and the vehicle that we've all ridden on, this media frenzy, this feeding frenzy, how the media will handle that, or whether they'll move onto new bait."

Appropriately enough for a man putting up a good display of not wanting to hand his soul over to the plastic wrappers, Beatles-wiggers, media frenzy generators and gastropublicans, one of the future fixtures in Law's career diary is a return to the stage, playing the title role in Marlowe's *Dr Faustus* at the Young Vic. Any father who, like Jude's, eats chocolate as if it's rationed would have to be approving of that.

His other approaching commitments appear equally judicious. In Sam "*American Beauty*" Mendes' next film, *The Road To Perdition*, he plays a crime scene photographer obsessed with taking the perfect still of a dead body. Tom Hanks and Paul Newman star with him. All quality work; all seemingly the right stuff to fend off DiCaprio-isation.

If Law is right and 1945 has continued to shape the culture long after we thought the effects had ebbed, feeding back into the idealism of the '60s and colouring attitudes to contemporary, corporate-industrial celebrity, he's probably one of the best advertisements for his own theory. History, see, hasn't let go of Jude - Jude and his principles: never moving to LA; giving good theatre; fed up with the paparazzi; pushing his family baby carrier away from the burning lights. He seems constructively grounded. Either way, he's a very fine actor.

"If you didn't act what would you do?" asks Robinson.

"I dunno," shrugs Jude.

"Was acting always on the cards?"

"Yeah, really. I remember being six doing stuff at school. It was the only thing that made sense. Even though my parents were teachers, they were into amateur dramatics. I just thought I loved that world, where kids are talking to adults, and adults are talking about things, having arguments and shouting, pretending to be pissed. It was so abstract, and so not normal, I just knew I wanted in on that.

"Mind you I envy you. I'm also one of those people that are perpetually looking at the other crafts in that world, like writing or directing. That's just me being restless. It's finding your role in that world, I suppose."

"Writing, acting and directing are very similar," suggests Robinson.

"My sister always read loads more than me, and she kind of encouraged me to read," says Jude. "When she was reading Bruce Chatwin, she tried to explain to me that he didn't write for an audience, and that's the best way to write - for yourself - and if someone chooses to read it that's great. I never really got that, but I think I kinda get it now, because you can't really act for your audience. You've got to act because you want to find out something about yourself.

"It's funny, because I wasn't really extrovert as a kid. It was more like a confidence. I was never the funny kid. I just felt like I knew what I wanted to do and I don't really suffer fools particularly. I don't really like people who bullshit and I don't like sheep."

"I can't stand fucking bullshit. Which is another thing I don't like about the industry," says Robinson.

"It's the fake friendship as well, that's what I don't like," agrees Jude. "One of the things that I really like about work, is being told that I'm wrong and I don't mind saying, 'I don't know what you mean,' but I don't like that thing in real life, when you can't see the person you're talking to because you know you're being fed it through a meat grinder. I can't bear that."

"But the more famous you get, the more frightening you get, and the more it is unlikely that people will tell you things," Robinson points out. "It'll be like, 'Oh, you can't say that to Jude.' I had a girlfriend, an actress - Leslie-Ann Downe. We went out to dinner with Peter Sellers one night, and I was saying something to him, and I'm not a loud-mouth but I just say what I think, and she's behind his head going... (makes 'Shut up!' gestures)..."

"He probably hadn't heard that in 20 years!" laughs Jude.

"He had some sort of talent didn't he? But God, he was a manic depressive. He had to be the epicentre, the axle, of the world. It's that old AA expression: 'I was the shit around which the Universe was created.'"

"I don't understand that side of it either," confides Jude. "I feel more than comfortable with a light shining in my face, and a room full of people all looking saying, 'Right, it's your turn. ACTION!' Or an audience staring at me when it's my turn to be Giovanni or Benvolio or whoever. But I don't want to be the centre of attention. That, I never understand. That must come from a deep insecurity actually. Maybe the reason I pissed people off as a kid was because I was happy not to be that. I think that sometimes challenges people. I'd rather not be that centre of attention ◼

WRITER, FATHER, BULLSHIT DETECTOR, BRUCE ROBINSON IS 54 YEARS YOUNG. ACTOR, FATHER, THEORIST AND CIRCUMSPECT STAR, JUDE LAW IS 28; BUT THAT'S IN OLD PUB, OLD SCHOOL, WAY-OLD SOUL YEARS.

MARIANNE

JACKET BY **VIKTOR & ROLF**; TROUSERS BY **HELMUT LANG**; TOP BY **KATAYONE ADELI**; LACE TOP BY **JANET REGER**; SHOES BY **CHRISTIAN LOUBOUTIN**.

INTERVIEW **BARNEY HOSKYNS**
PORTRAITS **HORST DIEKGERDES**
STYLING **NANCY ROHDE**
HAIR **ADAM BRYANT** FOR **TONY & GUY**
MAKE-UP **LIZ DAXAUER** USING **CALVIN KLEIN COSMETICS**
RETOUCHING **SHOEMAKERS ELVES**
PROCESSING **METRO STUDIOS**
PHOTOGRAPHIC ASSISTANCE **SANDRA FREIJ** AND **MARCUS PALMQUIS**
STYLING ASSISTANCE **VICTORIA YOUNG**

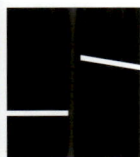

he was the posh blonde who fell in with a gang of blues-worshipping droogs, the "Naked Girl At Stones Party" of '60s Mars-bar infamy. She topped the pop charts then fell from grace, sliding into the twilight half-life of heroin addiction. Against the odds, Marianne Faithfull re-emerged at the end of the '70s with *Broken English*: a shocking statement of defiance sung in the harsh, hard-won voice of survival. Two decades on, Faithfull is more than a mere icon. She's a widely respected artist whose legend continues to influence pop's cutting edge. Which explains why Beck and Pulp have contributed to the making of her new album.

On the top floor of a Georgian townhouse in Dublin, a punt away from the Lansdowne Road rugby stadium, one of rock 'n' roll's greatest female icons is bending down to check on the rack of lamb roasting in the oven.

She's shoeless in a denim skirt, very blonde and voluptuous. She's loosened by a couple of glasses of the "very good red wine" delivered to her by film director Patrice Chereau (Faithfull co-stars in Chereau's latest film, *Intimacy*, which won the Best Film Award at this year's Berlin Film Festival).

Marianne Faithfull sweeps through her apartment, past a vast tome of Helmut Newton photographs on a waist-high lectern. The book is open at a portrait of herself, taken two years ago in Monte Carlo. "Oh, not again" she groans. "I always turn it to another page and Angie [her housekeeper] always turns it back." Back in the kitchen, with a sunset-streaked sky fading behind her, Faithfull talks about how she moved to Dublin from Shell Cottage, the rural folly that was her home for the better part of ten years. "I have what I call house luck," she pauses as if to consider, "Never had any man luck, but I always had house luck!"

Not that she wouldn't sometimes prefer to be closer to the glamour axis of London-Paris-New York. "I'd *love* the money to have a flat in Paris, but I *don't*," she says. "And I can live better here than I could in New York or London or Paris." At 54, what Marianne would like more than anything is the money to buy, rather than merely rent, a flat. "It would be nice," she smiles, "to make enough money not to have to totter on stage at 80."

The centrepiece of Faithfull's new album is "Sliding Thru Life On Charm", a song written for her by Jarvis Cocker - just one of several, young-ish, male admirers who've contributed to this remarkable record. The result is a song that distils the narrative of her life down to four superb verses:

In proper homes throughout the land/ Fathers try to understand/Why Eunice who is 17/ Aspires to live her live like me.

For Faithfull, "Sliding Thru" is an uncanny encapsulation of her life and the mythology surrounding it, a song she feels she could never have written herself. "When I first heard it I was stunned," she says. "In fact, I couldn't even imagine myself singing it. It took me a year before I understood it enough to record it. With this record, that was the first song I got and I've managed to build everything ➤

"WE WANTED TO MAKE A REALLY FUCKED-UP CLUB TRACK THAT WASN'T TRYING TOO HARD, AND DIDN'T SOUND TOO READY FOR THE RAVE CHAMBER"- Beck

> around it like a beautiful jewel."

"The catalyst was our very final appearance on *TFI Friday*, on which she was playing with Metallica," remembers Cocker. "She kind of collared me and said, 'Why don't you write a song for me?' And I said, 'I will if you give me a title'. And then I just went off with a copy of her autobiography, *Faithfull*, and underlined key passages. From that I found out a lot more about where she was actually coming from - the myth that she was from an aristocratic family and very well-off, and the fallacy of the Mars Bar episode. So it got me thinking about the fact that she represents a certain kind of fallen angel."

"Sliding Thru" also spells out the fact that Marianne has become a role model for today's pop generation. "There's a sort of revenge aspect to it that I like," Cocker says. "She's much more appealing to younger people than someone like, say, Cilla Black. I mean, do you wanna be Cilla Black or do you wanna be Marianne Faithfull? It's not a very difficult choice. And I hope the song really comes across as a real two-fingers up to people."

"She's extremely generous, kind and interested and very easy to work with," adds Beck. "She said she had a naughty sex song for me. I guess we both have an affinity for Serge Gainsbourg and his particular brand of licentiousness. She showed me the lyrics and I immediately knew what kind of track I wanted to create. We wanted to make a really fucked-up club track that wasn't trying too hard, and didn't sound too ready for the rave chamber."

No doubt it was "Sliding Thru", along with tracks such as Beck's electro-funk gem "Sex with Strangers", that helped Marianne sign a worldwide deal with Virgin Records. The deal has just been agreed when we meet in London a week later and Faithfull looks happy.

"This is the first time that I've had a real *push*," she says. "*Broken English* was a push, but it could have been better. It was an underground hit. I did receive a $90,000 royalty cheque after *Broken English*, but that was it. And I spent it in three months on drugs and clothes."

She talks about the illustrious line-up of Faithfull devotees who've contributed to the album. In addition to Beck and Cocker there's Billy Corgan (providing the rapturous, keyboard-swathed "I'm on Fire") and Damon Albarn (whose "Kissin' Time" won't be recorded until after our conversation). A stellar assembly of boys in thrall to the legend of... what, exactly? Marianne as Muse? Marianne as the *Girl On A Motorcycle*? Marianne as the Object who, became a Subject? "In the sense that I was a muse to Mick Jagger, which is a wonderful thing to be, or to Bob Dylan, which is also a wonderful thing to be, I don't know," Marianne says. "I'm very different to how they imagine me to be... and that's great, because they can work with me. It makes it fun for them to have someone who understands what they're saying. I'm not sure if that image of me from the past would have been something they could work with."

For Faithfull, the album is simultaneously a celebration of her legend and a collaboration with a group of artists who treat her as an equal.

"Everybody working on this record has a certain aesthetic and attitude to life itself that chimes with mine," she says. "It's collaboration from the heart, with people who would really understand who 'Marianne Faithfull' is and what they can do with her. Because that is the problem. The core problem is that I *didn't* slide through life on charm."

For many, Marianne Faithfull's story is the tale of a bright and beautiful girl who veered violently between roles: chanteuse and muse, diva and object of desire. As her old friend Pamela Mayall put it in *Dreaming My Dreams*, the '99 documentary about Faithfull's life, "She was both the glamorous star and the girl on Mick's arm."

"The boys are still looking for the same type of woman: the models, the blondes," says Marianne's contemporary, and fellow Stones muse, Anita Pallenberg. "It just happens that among those women there are a few intelligent ones."

"We both had real culture, and that was a very interesting element to bring to the Stones," adds Faithfull. "It's a wonderful gig to be a muse. It's incredibly ego-enhancing, but it's not something we set out to do. Anita certainly wasn't >

MARIANNE FAITHFULL DISCOGRAPHY

2000 TRUE: THE COLLECTION
'99 VAGABOND WAYS
'98 APERFECT STRANGER
'98 SEVEN DEADLY SINS
'97 20TH CENTURY BLUES
'95 A SECRET LIFE
'90 BLAZING AWAY
'87 STRANGE WEATHER
'87 VERY BEST OF MARIANNE FAITHFULL
'84 RICH KID BLUES
'84 SUMMER NIGHTS
'83 A CHILD'S ADVENTURE
'81 DANGEROUS ACQUAINTANCES
'81 AS TEARS GO BY
'79 BROKEN ENGLISH
'78 FAITHLESS
'78 DREAMING MY DREAMS
'69 THE WORLD OF MARIANNE FAITHFULL
'67 LOVE IN A MIST
'66 FAITHFUL FOREVER
'66 NORTH COUNTRY MAID
'65 GO AWAY FROM MY WORLD
'65 COME MY WAY
'65 MARIANNE FAITHFULL

FILMOGRAPHY

2001 INTIMACY, THE CHIEFTAINS - THE LONG BLACK VEIL
'95 MOONDANCE
'96 ABSOLUTELY FABULOUS - "THE LAST SHOUT!" (TV)
'93 SHOPPING
'90 KENNETH ANGER - LUCIFER RISING
'90 MARIANNE FAITHFULL - BLAZING AWAY
'90 ROGER WATERS - THE WALL LIVE IN BERLIN
'75 ASSAULT ON AGATHON
'75 GHOST STORY: MADHOUSE MANSION
'69 HAMLET
'68 ROLLING STONES, THE - ROCK AND ROLL CIRCUS
'68 GIRL ON A MOTORCYCLE
'67 I'LL NEVER FORGET WHAT'S 'ISNAME

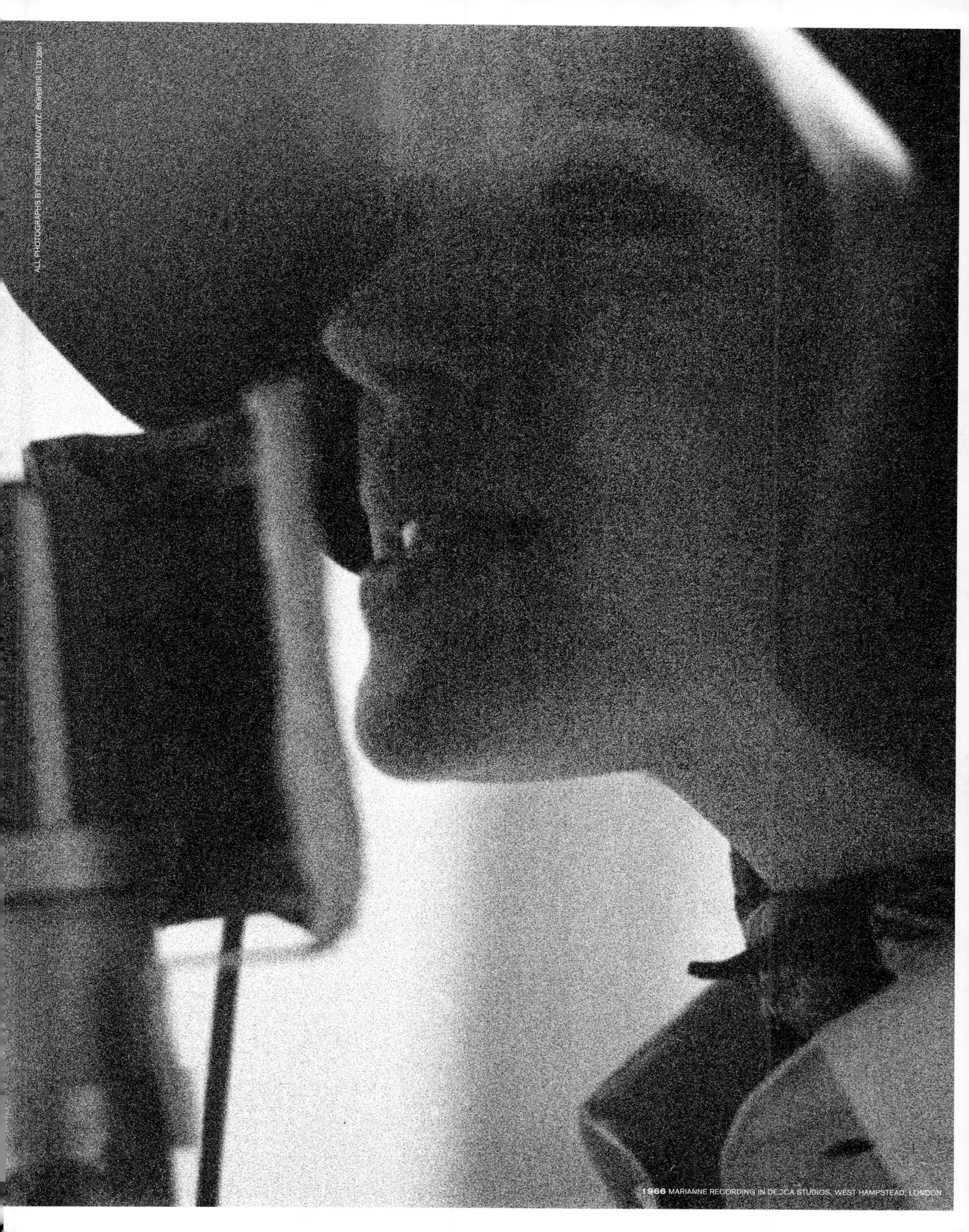

1966 MARIANNE RECORDING IN DECCA STUDIOS, WEST HAMPSTEAD, LONDON

> careerist about it. The thing about the really interesting women is that they don't actually care that much."

However, just as rock'n'roll wasn't ready for Janis Joplin, so it wasn't ready for a strong woman who broke free of her day-job as Rolling Stones' consort.

"One of the reasons I didn't get a band together in 1970 *was* Janis's death," Marianne admits. "That long, long gap between 'Sister Morphine' and *Broken English* wasn't necessary. But when the news came in about Janis... I just gave up. She was a sacrifice to society's vision of women, and I got scared."

The irony that "Sister Morphine" - the song she wrote with Mick Jagger and recorded with the late Jack Nitzsche in '69 - has earned her more money than any of her other compositions is not lost on Faithfull. But it was the Stones version (for *Sticky Fingers* when Marianne was already a junkie living on the streets of Soho) which kept the cash coming.

And yet Faithfull had been a *bona fide* '60s star, chalking up a string of hits that began with Mick and Keith's folk-pop ballad "As Tears Go By". "Her life gets concertinaed into heroin overdoses in a poor choice of location and an affinity for Mars bars as opposed to Sunday tea," notes Andrew Loog Oldham, the manager/ svengali who first clocked her at a "Swinging London" party in early '64. "The fact is forgotten that Marianne had, between August '64 and July '65, four Top 10 hits in the UK."

Oldham is rightly proud of his work with a woman he recognised as his intellectual equal. He also believes Marianne was a victim of the way he sold her to the British public - as an aristocratic nymph who'd somehow strayed into a career as a pop songbird. And the denouement of all this is, of course, the punishment and excoriation resulting from her (mis)adventures with the Stones - above all the infamous drug bust at Keith Richards Sussex home in February '67.

"The real joke is that I didn't fall into pop music by accident, I just made it look as if I did," she laughs with perhaps just the faintest trace of bitterness. "If I hadn't really wanted to do it, my mother would never have signed a contract with Decca or with Andrew. Since I was eight, I'd

had singing lessons, piano lessons, everything. I *fell into* pop music maybe before I was ready, in fact while I was still technically a child."

What Marianne couldn't do in the '60s was make that voice heard in its raw honest state. She couldn't be a posh rock chick *and* a singer-songwriter with her own story to tell. Like Pallenberg (companion first to Brian Jones and then more famously to Keith Richards), she wanted to get into the boys room and see what they were doing. Also like Pallenberg, when she'd served her purpose as the trophy she was very effectively erased from the Stones' inner circle.

Marianne's period as an "exile" on Main Street (or at least on the streets of '70s Soho) is one of the central elements of her legend. And how she survived her own calculated self-annihilation through addiction, a coldly rational act based mainly on her reading of *The Naked Lunch,* is the fundamental backdrop to "Sliding Thru Life On Charm".

Go ahead, why don't you leave me to these thugs/And creeps who wanna fuck a nun on drugs/Is it such a sin, I never even tried too hard/I had to know how far was going too far...

"I really just wanted to disappear," Marianne remembers of her decision to become a junkie. "I had a vague idea that the only way out of it was complete surrender. And I did that - I took an enormous chance, really, that by going down as far as I could go I would fall through the bottom and come out into the light. And that's what happened."

When producer Mike Leander tracked her down in Soho in '72 - the resulting album, *Rich Kid Blues,* would not see the light till many years later. Faithfull had given up on her career as a singer. "It's quite chilling to think that a woman at 26 could think that her life was over."

In '75, a Nashville ballad Marianne recorded for the NEMS label, "Dreaming My Dreams", suddenly and unexpectedly took off in Ireland. The song reached No.1, becoming a metaphorical anthem about the troubles and cementing her relationship with the Emerald Isle. "I come from that space," she laughs. "My

job is to sell records and have hits. That's what I want. And I got one here. And they're very, very cool, very nice people." Faithfull realised she might have something to say after all. Still in the grip of addiction, she groped her way towards recording *Broken English,* piecing together a band and assembling the songs - the characters - that appear on that startling album: John Lennon's "Working-Class Hero", Dr Hook's "Lucy Jordan", the green-eyed Fury of Heathcote Williams' "Why D'Ya Do It?", the Ulrike Meinhof of the album's ominous, title track. All these figures - like the fey maiden created by Oldham, like her Ophelia in Tony Richardson's '69 production of *Hamlet,* like her Lilith in Kenneth Anger's notorious film *Lucifer Rising* - were masks for Marianne herself, versions of the anguished but unleashed woman she'd become.

Few could forget the shock of hearing *Broken English* the first time - hearing that sardonic yet soulful contralto, a voice of dreadful experience if not of death itself. "When Marianne sings it sounds like she hasn't slept since '66," says Dave Stewart, who co-wrote the new album's "Song for Nico" - a tribute of sorts to a woman hell-bent on self-annihilation. "It's as though each word has been chiselled out of a huge piece of cocaine she's been trying to dispose of but just won't go away."

"It was such a shock hearing *Broken English,*" adds Kate Hyman, who worked for Marianne as a teenager and who was recently responsible for signing multi-platinum dance deity Moby. "The first taste of Marianne was this pure, sweet voice in the '60s, and here she was suddenly as this powerful interpreter of songs."

This was not - and still isn't - a rock voice, a Janis Joplin. As befitting the daughter of Austro-Jewish baroness Eva von Sacher-Masoch (and the great-great-niece of the man who wrote *Venus In Furs,* no less), it was a cabaret croak closer to Dagmar Krause or the wracked cry of Billie Holiday's final records.

"It was 'Woman Is The Nigger Of The World'," Marianne says of Billie Holiday's voice. "That is exactly what I heard, and what I knew. I'd read *The Second Sex* while I was still at school, but ➤

JULY 5, 1969 MICK JAGGER ON STAGE IN HYDE PARK JUST AFTER THE DEATH OF BRIAN JONES

1980 LEAVING HER FULHAM FLAT

1967

1968 MARIANNE IN "ROCK 'N' ROLL CIRCUS"

1965 IN DECCA STUDIOS, WEST HAMPSTEAD WHILST RECORDING "COME MY WAY"

> "WHEN SHE SINGS IT'S AS THOUGH EACH WORD HAS BEEN CHISELLED OUT OF A HUGE PIECE OF COCAINE SHE'S BEEN TRYING TO DISPOSE OF BUT JUST WON'T GO AWAY"
> - Dave Stewart

› when I read *The Female Eunuch*, it was after *that* that I realised I had to walk out [on Mick Jagger]. I'm sure I recognised what I did in the Germaine Greer book because of what I'd already known intuitively from Billie Holiday and Bessie Smith."

Anita Pallenberg called her friend "a punk diva", and not even the *Broken English* typically tasteful production can conceal the scars perceptible on the new album. Punk certainly embraced Marianne, encouraging her to sink further into heroin addiction. "I wore seditionaries clothes," she recalls of the era. "I lived in a basement in Lots Road [Chelsea] and you can't get much more punk than that." Married in November '79 to her bass player, ex-Vibrator Ben Brierley, Faithfull managed to keep her band on the road through '81's slick, synthy *Dangerous Acquaintances*. "There were some really heavy times, but I don't think I've met anyone as strong as Marianne," attests guitarist Barry Reynolds, her musical linchpin for nearly 25 years. "And she is one of the funniest people I've met." By the time of *A Child's Adventure* ('83), Faithfull was at large in the rotten core of New York City, strung out and gasping for air. Songs like "Times Square" and "Running For Our Lives" were naked cries for help - unanswered until her friend Tom Hayes persuaded her to seek treatment at Minnesota's Hazelden Institute in '85. That same year, finally, Marianne kicked both her habit and her second marriage.

"There's a hell of a lot of heroin in Dublin, but I don't know about it," Marianne Faithfull informs me breezily. "I have no experience of that in my life here, and never have had. I have one or two friends in London who do heroin, but I hardly ever see them. It's one of my benchmarks. Coke freaks too. I don't really want them around. All of these things are incredibly irrelevant if you're not interested in them." We're reclining in the cosy living room of her Dublin apartment, listening to a selection of tracks from Harry Smith's landmark *Anthology Of American Folk Music*. Some of these she's about to sing at a show honouring Smith, staged in Los Angeles by her old friend and producer (*Strange Weather*, *Blazing Away*) Hal Wilner. Her favourite is Blind Willie Johnson's "John the Revelator".

A little later, a rough mix of "Sliding Thru Life on Charm" blasts through her speakers. "I don't know if anyone is even interested," Marianne says coyly of her album. "I hope they are. It's going to take a *lotta* work, and a *lotta* marketing." She talks like the old pro she's become - the haughty singer of Brecht/Weill songs on *20th Century Blues* and the splendid artist of *The Seven Deadly Sins*. She's the woman whom David Dalton ("ghost" writer of *Faithfull*) describes as "the caretaker of her own legend". She talks feistily, too, of the film of her life that Jim (*In The Name Of The Father*) Sheridan is supposed to have finished writing. "Jim's not got his shit together, and my rights come back to me in October. I like him as a friend, but that's got nothing to do with it. Business is business, and this has to get made... Because then I can buy my flat. It's the most amount of money I'll ever see in my life." Faithfull's impatience disguises the fact that more than anything she thrives on performance which is why, the long and tiring flight notwithstanding, she's looking forward to the Harry Smith show in LA. "I love America, because the people there really get my work," she says. "It's also why I go to Australia. When Marianne Faithfull steps onto the stage in Sydney, *they* know, and *I* know... and they *know* I know... that they saved my life." This is Faithfull's sole reference to the suicide attempt she made down-under while filming Tony Richardson's *Ned Kelly* with Mick Jagger. (You can almost hear Helen Mirren speaking these words in the finished Marianne Faithfull biopic:) In *Dreaming My Dreams*, as Marianne laps up the applause at the end of her '89 show in St Anne's Cathedral, Brooklyn, she thanks the audience: "I *really needed* this. Coz ya *never* fuckin' know, and I *need* to know..." She knows now ▌▎

BARNEY HOSKYNS IS THE EDITOR OF ROCK'S BACKPAGES WWW.ROCKSBACKPAGES.COM AND IS AUTHOUR OF *ACROSS THE GREAT DIVIDE - THE BAND AND AMERICA*, *SAY IT ONE TIME FOR THE BROKENHEARTED - COUNTRY SOUL IN THE AMERICAN SOUTH* AND *WAITING FOR THE SUN*.
PORTRAITS SHOT AT **KEW GARDENS**, LONDON +44 20 8332 5568 WITH THANKS TO LUKE FULL AND TOM HOBLYN.

CHANEL

26 OLD BOND STREET • 167-170 SLOANE STREET
HARRODS • HEATHROW TERMINALS 3 AND 4
OPENING AUTUMN 2001 AT BROMPTON CROSS

FROM CROUCHING TIGERS TO HIDDEN VIRUSES,
EVOLUTION HAS THROWN UP MANIFOLD EXAMPLES OF
CAMOUFLAGE AND MIMICRY IN THE NATURAL WORLD,
BUT NONE AS SPECTACULAR AS THE MIMIC OCTOPUS.

NATURAL ACTOR

PHOTOGRAPHY **LARRY AND DENISE TACKETT**
TEXT **CALLUM MCGEOCH**

1 C

1 B

It comes as no surprise to learn that nature's unmatched master of disguise has eluded scientific discovery until only recently. Indeed, the provisionally named 1) mimic octopus is still waiting official classification.

First sighted by marine photographers, Roger Stein and Rudie Kuiter in a bay off the island of Flores east of Java, Indonesia, the news of an octopus that was believed to be mimicking a flatfish, as well as A) a sea snake, spread quickly through the marine biological community. Already responsible for identifying and describing over 150 new octopus species in his short career, young Australian expert Mark Norman wanted to be among the first to witness this exciting new discovery. Taking Roger and Rudie back with him, as well as a BBC TV crew led by the highly experienced filmmaker Joe Kennedy, Mark set off for Flores. Unfortunately, the area of the original sighting had since been completely obliterated by a devastating combination of a cyclone and an earthquake. Instead the team headed for a bay of similar positioning and topography in nearby Sulawesi, in hope of studying and filming the mimic for the first time.

The scientific viewpoint that a creature doesn't exist until someone with the right qualifications has made an official classification can become absurd, particularly when the local community have been aware of an "unrecognised" species for generations. In the case of mimic octopus, when, after five weeks without success, the crew decided to ask the Indonesian locals if they recognised the creature in the photographs, the first word they said was "bagus" which roughly translates as "mmm tasty". With the locals confirming what they already suspected about the mimic's preferred habitat - flat, silty seabed at around 10 metres depth - the team set off with renewed enthusiasm. Finally, less than a week before they were due to return, they found a mimic octopus in Totok Bay, Teluk, Sulawesi. In fact they almost dropped their anchor directly on top of one.

Over the following days of extended filming, what they observed went far beyond what even the remarkable photos had promised. The team watched in wonder as the octopus swam along the seabed in smooth undulations, its legs folded behind, exactly like a flounder. Then with all but two legs hidden in its lair it did an uncanny impersonation of a venomous, banded sea snake, just as Roger and Rudie had described. But then, the longer they watched and saw it confronted by different potential threats, they identified many more, highly varied imitations. "He'd stare and watch us and then eventually he'd relax and go about his business," remembers Joe. "When surprised, it would switch suddenly from, say, a flounder to B) a lionfish, stiffening his tentacles to resemble the long poisonous spines."

In total they saw the mimic morph fluidly through at least 15 different recognisable disguises, including a sting ray, a sand anemone, a mantis shrimp, a ghost crab, C) a brittlestar, a hermit crab, a jawfish and a blenny using subtle changes in arm posture, colour patterns and swimming motion.

"What was so fascinating to watch was the speed with which it could change its colour and its shape," Joe recalls. "Without a skeleton it seems almost anything is possible. But perhaps most striking is not just the physical changes it makes, but also its behavioural changes. It moves its body in very different ways, depending on the creature it's mimicking." After looking at further specimens to corroborate their observations, the team realised, after some confusion, that they were actually looking at two species. The second, which has been provisionally christened Wonderpuss, looks almost identical to the mimic and also has a repertoire of impersonations; but nothing compared to the theatrical range and delightful thespian flourishes of the real star - the mimic octopus.

One problem that the research, so far, has yet to solve is whether the mimic's incredible acting talent is something it's born with or a set of skills acquired as it develops. And if it's the latter, as they only live for around one year, do they have to learn fast or do they teach each other? Nothing can be ruled out.

Right now, the mimic octopus' star is still very much in the ascendant. Luxury hotels and dive centres from Thailand to the Phillipines now advertise Wonderpuss and the mimic as their star attractions regardless of whether there is any realistic chance of seeing them or not.

The resulting increase in marine tourism, combined with heavy fishing pressures is making Mark Norman's ongoing mission to identify and protect new octopus species in the Indo-Malayan archipelago all the more urgent; it could soon be too late ■

1   A

THEY MAY BE UNKNOWN, BUT MARK THESE FOUR NAMES FOR AN OFF SCHEDULE TREAT IN NEW YORK.

PHOTOGRAPHY **MICHAEL EVANET**
AT **LIGHTHOUSE USA**
COORDINTATION **J J FARRAR**
PRODUCTION **VANESSA HODGE** AT
LIGHTHOUSE USA
THANKS TO **MERCEDES-BENZ, LTI, TOMMY** AND
BILLY AT SUPERIOR DELI, QUEENS

There was a time when the New York collections were about flying in on a Wednesday morning, catching Ralph, Donna and Calvin over the next couple of days then flying out again for a weekend break before heading straight for Milan and Paris - where the *real* fashion was. The Seventh Avenue giants are, of course, more than adept at issuing their twice-yearly - and predictable - trend statements with clothes that are safe, easy to wear and beautifully (read expensively) produced. But they are hardly likely to throw up anything much that's new.

Fast forward to autumn 2001 and, in terms of fashion, New York City is a rather different place to be. Since labels as diverse as Imitation Of Christ and Miguel Adrover appeared on the scene, sending out hugely individual clothes that they refused to show in the sterile environs of the tents in Bryant Park, the way seems to have been paved for a whole new wave of designers. From Alice Roi to Ben Cho and from Tawfik Mounayer to Bruce, designers seem intent on creating something new, and proud to wear their multi-cultural mix on their sleeve ▪

LEFT TO RIGHT: MAN ON PHONE, TAWFIK MOUNAYER; SEATED, ALICE ROI; STANDING, BEN CHO, NICOLE NOSELLI AND DAPHNE GUTIEREZ OF BRUCE.
SEE STOCKISTS PAGE FOR DESIGNER CONTACT DETAILS

MARC JACOBS

MARC JACOBS

PERFUME

MARC JACOBS

MARC JACOBS
SHOES

MARC JACOBS

BAGS

MARC JACOBS
PERFUME

MARC JACOBS
PERFUME

MARC JACOBS

SOFIA COPPOLA, HANNELORE KNUTS, STEPHEN MALKMUS, STEPHANIE SEYMOUR, TASHA TILBERG
PHOTOGRAPHED BY JUERGEN TELLER

COLLECTIONS REPORT

The autumn/winter 2001 season will go down in fashion history as being about as contrary as a petulant child. The battle will be a ferocious one - there's nothing much like a fashion spat after all - between the vampish and the plain pretty, the masculine and the overtly feminine, the sophisticated and the sweetly naive.

At Gucci, there was skin-tight black tailoring gleaming with zips that snaked from throat to waistline and from waist-line to hem one minute, a parade of what can only be described as baby doll dresses the next. At Alexander McQueen, where a Victorian toyshop formed the backdrop and an art deco merri-go-round took centre stage, models stalked out in everything from frilly lace ra-ra skirts to World War I, Kaiser Willhelm helmets and floor-sweeping black leather greatcoats.

"I wanted to explore the sinister side of childhood as well as the fun," McQueen said after his show - the soundtrack sampled the eerie voiceover of the Chitty Chitty Bang Bang childcatcher and many of the looks were inspired by the film but this was infant fantasy at its most twisted. "They show children clowns as if they're funny. They're not, they're really scary."

Christian Dior, too, encapsulated extreme contrasts in mood: mannish tailoring was juxtaposed with quite the prettiest floral-print, bias-cut sheath dresses in a show that was pure Galliano at his most insanely eclectic. At Comme des Garçons, meanwhile, win-some lace-trimmed dresses, layered one over the other, were cinched at the waist with glossy black weightlifters' belts. Suffice it to say that a petticoat has never looked so, well, so hard.

With the typical reticence to expand on her vision that belies her stature as perhaps the world's greatest designer, Rei Kawakubo said that her collection was about "freedom beyond the taboo, expressed in the Comme des Garçons way". Trousers slashed at the crotch - for easy access, perhaps? - certainly put the wind up the more politically correct in attendance. But, then, this is fashion, those who take offence easily might do well to look away.

As if to drive fashion's current, disparate nature home, even the requisite revivals came, this season, from opposing

FENDI Karl Lagerfeld revisited the optimistic futurism of the '60s and Courrèges in particular.

ALEXANDER MCQUEEN Floor-sweeping, black leather great coats and World War I, Kaiser Willhelm helmets made for a look that's as strict and hard as it gets.

YVES SAINT LAURENT Tom Ford preferred to plunder the wasp-waisted, full-skirted silhouette of the Victorian era for this show.

Fashion mayhem !...

corners: the dark, repressed sexuality of the Victorian era on the one hand and the happy optimism of the free-loving '60s youthquake on the other. It seems strange to some, incidentally, that in our proud to be modern times, there are always revivals. At Christian Dior, John Galliano went out on a limb and revisited the Acid House movement of the early '90s - and this not even a decade after the original was laid to rest. This made for uncomfortable viewing for those old enough to have lived through "smiley culture" the first time round - memories of drug-fuelled escapades in muddy fields, located around the none-too-glamorous M25, continue to make the thirtysomething generation wince in pain. It is interesting, however, that for younger members of Galliano's privileged audience, this was a blithe and brightly coloured sight for fashion eyes. The fact that the great names in fashion seem, for the time being at least, to have agreed to disagree is, of course, just as it should be. It almost goes without saying that the days when girls will be girls are long gone, and among the greatest things about being a woman at the turn of the 21st century is that fashion can be dictatorial only at its own expense. In the end women wear what they want to wear and are quite empowered enough to step out in corsets and stilettos should they so wish - let anyone tell them they can't wear them to the office at their peril. Equally, should they prefer a more androgynous low-profile dress solution, that's fine too. The cleverly post-modern, meanwhile, will really put the cat among the pigeons by mixing the two. This - alongside the requisite jeans-and-t-shirt combination that no modern woman, or indeed man, should ever be without - is, perhaps, the most contemporary way of them all to dress.

In a world where the mega-corporation reigns supreme - news of The Gucci Group snapping up one name after another in lethal competition with France's giant LVMH breaks almost daily - individuality shone like the brightest of lights at the collections. There are certain designers who, quite refreshingly, remain true to their own particular vision whether this fits neatly into any prevailing trend or not.

In New York Miguel Adrover sent out floor-length caftans, harem pants and layered printed tunics, all of which went to prove that there is more to looking lovely than a mini-skirt and high heels. ▸

CHRISTIAN DIOR The most feminine, floral-print chiffon sheath dresses were finished with ultra-romantic, gypsy headscarves.

MIGUEL ADROVER Individuality shone like the brightest of lights for this collection inspired by the Egyptian countryside.

GUCCI Mannish tailoring embellished with zips were swiftly followed by a selection of girlie baby doll dresses.

CHRISTIAN LACROIX A rainbow-coloured collection by a maximal designer now ripe for revival.

It's been quite some time, since fashion shed its overtly sexed up image in favour of something rather more demure, dignified even. Adrover spent six weeks travelling in Egypt, by all accounts, living with a family in the countryside for three of them. This clearly threw up inspirational references and a collection that had unusual emotional power and warmth.

In London individuality ruled the day across the board. The designers who show in the British fashion capital are exceptionally young and, often, unformed but live by the belief that any idea is a good idea - which at least makes for stimulating viewing, if not always great clothes. Russell Sage and Boudicca both came into their own this season, the former having refined his vintage-fabric inspired, deconstructed then reconstructed vision, the latter paring ideas down to more simple and modern effect. New names vying for the somewhat dubious Next Big Thing Award include Warren Noronha - formerly of the Antonio Berardi stable - and Hamish Morrow, a designer whose black lace dresses, hand-finished almost to couture standards stood out.

If London and, New York in particular, pointed at forthcoming trends, Milan did its best to hammer them home. The world was in no doubt, following the Italian collections, of the fact that the pretty dress is back on the map, but then so is masculine tailoring. A-line mini-dresses here, there and everywhere paid tribute to Courrèges and a '60s silhouette. Enough corsetry to make Paul Poiret spin in his grave reminded us that this is also a Moulin Rouge moment. This was, as always, a see and be seen occasion - the looks paraded by even the more low-key fashion editors were, quite often, more interesting than the shows themselves.

It was left to Paris, however, to ultimately save the sartorial day, simply by having it all. This is the only fashion capital in the world capable of turning out big ideas, backed up by equally beautiful clothes. Only in the French fashion capital are concepts quite so cleverly realised and designers so diverse. Perhaps that is because the mix of the modern and the traditional, the radical and the conservative is one that has been cultivated throughout fashion history. Which other place on the planet would be home to both that last bastion of bourgeois fashion, Chanel, and the louche monochromatic minimalism of Ann Demeulemeester? Where else in the world would the exuberant frivolity of Christian Lacroix rub shoulders with the dry and subversive wit of Viktor & Rolf? M Lacroix, incidentally, is a man ripe for revival. For the past few seasons, his collections have seemed rather too maximal for comfort. This is, after all, a designer who makes us ask: does a lilac fur jacket with oversized zebra collar and cuffs really need a fringe of rainbow-coloured mink tails and the odd fondant coloured pom-pom, or a pair of ruby-red sequinned trousers, their very own and equally vivid red chiffon veil? Colour, texture and print collided in this particular collection, as they say. Most lovely were tulle petticoat dresses densely covered with a patch-work of rainbow sequins and beads. If Lacroix has his way, we will all be wearing them come autumn with thigh-high suede boots in brightest lime, lemon, orange and turquoise.

Viktor & Rolf, conversely, showed a collection entirely in black, down to models' skin which was painted from crown to toe.

"A silhouette is an empty template, a mere black surface deprived of substance… Any object wrapped up in black cloth, or any drawing filled in with

COMME DES GARÇONS The pretty petticoat dress in bedroom colours has never looked so hard.

CHRISTIAN DIOR Are we ready to revisit "smiley culture" quite so soon? Monsieur Galliano thinks so, clearly.

YVES SAINT LAURENT The new granny boot is laced up to the thigh.

ANN DEMEULEMEESTER A designer true to herself and the resolutely louche, monochromatic vision that made her name.

VIKTOR & ROLF An inky black romp through the French 20th century fashion archives - from Balenciaga to Yves Saint Laurent.

ALEXANDER MCQUEEN Erin O'Connor as the world's saddest - and most lovely - clown dressed in narrow-waisted full-skirted black ballgown.

CHANEL A tweedy coat is pure, ladylike chic, finished with the postmodern logomania that now also characterises the label.

black ink transforms into an impenetrable surface. In that sense, the silhouette has the properties of a black hole, sucking in distinctions, details, and ultimately visibility."

Viktor & Rolf are not the first designers to use black to emphasise form and, in particular, silhouette at the expense of surface detail. In the early '80s Comme des Garçons and Yohji Yamamoto did just this, only exploding into colour ten years later, once the rest of the world had caught on. Concept aside, however, this was an accomplished and surprisingly commercial collection, comprising little pieces of French fashion history reworked for the 21st century and shown on what resembled nothing more than inky black mannequins. Here was the effortless style of the Chanel suit, right down to the pearls, black in this instance, of course; there was the liberating trouser suit for women that originally came courtesy of Yves Saint Laurent, the dramatic silhouettes of vintage Balenciaga and the exaggerated proportions of Dior's New Look. It all looked the epitome of Parisian chic, all too often strangely absent from the Paris collections, with just enough exaggeration of proportion - an overblown puffed sleeve, a huge black rose at the neckline of a perfectly simple jacket - to draw attention to the fact that these are, in fact, cool modern clothes generating from a cool modern design sensibility.

A rainbow-coloured bag of boiled sweets of a collection courtesy of Christian Lacroix, an inky black romp through the archives by Viktor & Rolf... Shown only hours - and streets - apart, both were utterly individual, lovely in their own entirely distinctive ways. This came as proof if ever any were needed, that opposites not only feed off one another, they really do attract.

... or just proof that opposites really do attract.

VICTORIANA

It is typical of fashion's perverse nature that, at the turn of the new millennium, designers continue to hark back to the Victorian era. Few working in the industry today could not be seduced by the technical brilliance - and macabre beauty - of corsets, crinolines and bustles, many of them more reminiscent of surgical instruments than anything more readily associated with clothing.

If fashion is about the transformation of the natural silhouette, then this is that concept's most extreme incarnation - a far cry from the low-slung, snake-hipped nonchalance that has dominated, on the runways and beyond, for so long. This, presumably, is also why it continues to fascinate.

McQueen always has a touch of the Victorian about his collections: the cruel but beautiful restriction of the wasp-waisted silhouette, suits his overall oeuvre; particularly the later s-line corsetry that travels right down over the hips, so that even now, with stretch fabrics, standing up or lying flat is the only viable option. This time round, however, a Victorian influence was more implied than literal - in the backdrop of a toyshop from that era - and in the form of Erin O'Connor who, dressed as the world's saddest and most sartorially accomplished clown, cut something of a dash in black lace ballgown with hugely overblown skirt. Think Scarlet O'Hara at her most Gothic.

The fact that Comme des Garçons' collection was rooted in this era was less predictable. As if in playful celebration of her 20th anniversary showing in Paris, the designer was in light-hearted spirits, this time turning her ability to deconstruct conventional clothing and transform it into something rather more interesting to the 19th century boudoir: specifically, corsetry and the kind of lace-trimmed lingerie that today is the preserve of the fevered male libido intent on unspeakable Valentine's Day festivities.

MOULIN ROUGE Nicole Kidman in the film du jour - she wore Yves Saint Laurent, a collection inspired by that era, to the film's premiere in Cannes.

VINTAGE CRINOLINE The Victorian underskirt looked more like a surgical instrument than conventional clothing.

COMME DES GARÇONS The corset turned on its head - here fused with men's tailoring - in a collection full of subversive wit.

The technical brilliance continues to inspire.

Tailored men's jackets metamorphosed, via the corset, into tiny mini-crinolines, their hems, referring back to menswear again, in grey flannel or box-pleated wool. Lace trimmed petticoat dresses in red, black, white and purple, with varying straps and necklines, were layered, one over the other. Trouser suits came with sheer black panels - a chevron of the type of heavy fabric used for structured underwear at the waist or just below the knee - and bra details revealed in panels cut out of the backs of jackets. Shorts looked deceptively simple from the front, but exploded into tennis knicker ruffles from behind. The shoes in the collection were more disco in flavour: gleaming black, ferociously pointed men's brogues complete with huge diamante buckles.

Ankle-length skirts with can-can frills, severe black coats with exaggerated skirts and even hybrid granny boots - laced up to the thigh - owed more than a little to Toulouse Lautrec and the Moulin Rouge at Yves Saint Laurent too. Small wonder that Nicole Kidman wore new season Saint Laurent to the film du jour's premiere in Cannes. Tom Ford, now in his second season presiding over the label, is rather too modern a designer to resort to costume, however. Rather, his greatest skill is to take references from the past and reinterpret them so they become far more than mere pastiche. In this case, inspiration also clearly came from Monsieur Saint Laurent's own gypsy collection - flocking at neckline and hips were one direct reference. The fusion between the two, with a little of Ford's own black-shirt-slashed-open-to-navel-style sex appeal thrown in for good measure, made for a glamour and ease that ensured this is a collection that will not only walk out of the shops but also be picked up by the high street even before the originals that inspired them make the rails.

Elsewhere, John Galliano deconstructed a leather biker jacket, transforming it into a corset/bustier top. Nicolas Ghesquiere at Balenciaga, meanwhile, proved himself, once again, a designer supremely comfortable with his references - few are able to load quite so much onto a garment while never apparently over-embellishing it. This time he put both the corset and crinoline under the microscope, using their linear structure in the form of surface detail on both shirts and miniskirts. Tight vests, in particular, created the illusion of corsetted silhouettes, as did skirts with exaggerated hips. Balenciaga is, unsurprisingly, still top of every fashion list worth reading for now: this was beautiful, with all the delicacy of antique anatomical drawing.

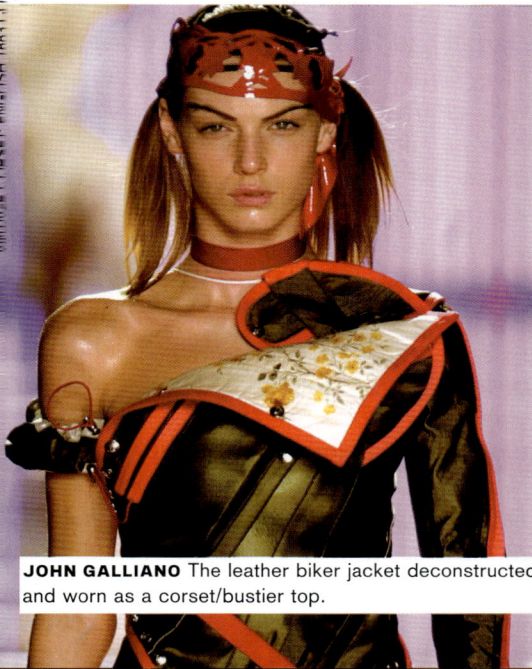

BALENCIAGA The illusion of the corset and crinoline is here created by embroidery, pleating and other surface detail.

JOHN GALLIANO The leather biker jacket deconstructed and worn as a corset/bustier top.

YVES SAINT LAURENT A mix of can-can frills, ruching from Saint Laurent's gypsy collection and slashed-to-the-navel sex appeal.

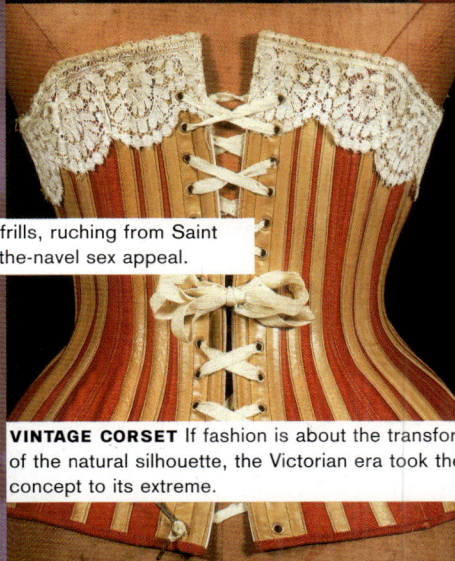

VINTAGE CORSET If fashion is about the transformation of the natural silhouette, the Victorian era took the concept to its extreme.

SCARLET O'HARA The Southern belle with the 18-inch waist continues to inspire - if in a rather more dark incarnation.

FUTURISM
- THE SIXTIES REVISITED

For spring/summer the miniskirt - '80s style - was offered up by designers the world over, hugging fashionable hips that felt, quite frankly, over-exposed after seasons of the knee-length A-line variety. Few over the age of 16, say, felt quite ready at first to travel the body-conscious, Azzedine Alaïa route once more. Fashion moves in mysterious - and fickle - ways, however, and now, with legs freshly buffed, anything even vaguely bell-shaped and/or knee-length makes those who care about such things feel like nothing more than the proverbial librarian.

For those in possession of gamine good looks and for whom the '80s was a little too overtly power fuelled, the '60s-line mini, inspired by Courrèges, Pierre Cardin and Paco Rabanne as well as by Mary Quant and the London youthquake will come as a breath of fresh fashion air. It has a minimal simplicity - particularly in dress form - that is far more in line with a modern aesthetic and is cutely coltish as opposed to in-your-face sexy.

If Junya Watanabe's rainbow-coloured tweed paid homage to the classic Chanel suit, the colours - think fondant brights - and straight-up, straight down silhouette was the stuff that made the likes of Twiggy and Jean Shrimpton famous. One after another - and sometimes in pairs - came basically the same outfit but with minute alterations in embellishment and cut to show just how accomplished a designer the Comme des Garçons protégé is in his own right. Back-combed beehives also harked back to the '60s in a less-than-literal fashion and a Courrèges reference came in the form of strips of Perspex running along ever more complex seams or cut out at the breast or nape of the neck.

Watanabe is not a man who is ever likely to dress the mainstream - that is not his position. He is, however, a true original and a designer who understands that, with the ubiquitous likes of Gucci, Prada and Chloé flooding the rails, the only way to really stand out in a crowd and/or push fashion forward is to take a more conceptual approach. The overall effect of his show was of an army of beautiful alien schoolgirls landing on our humble planet to show we lesser mortals how to dress. It was all far brighter, happier and less weighed down with the

ANNA SUI A little too literal, perhaps? The designer's models looked like they could have stepped out of the King's Road, c.1965.

CALVIN KLEIN The quintessential '90s minimalist is well suited to the pure line of a '60s revival.

MARY QUANT At the forefront of the youthquake that shook London and the world.

Look back to the future in a Courrèges moment.

FENDI A monochromatic palette, saucy, short silhouette and even bright, white go-go boots made this a Courrèges moment.

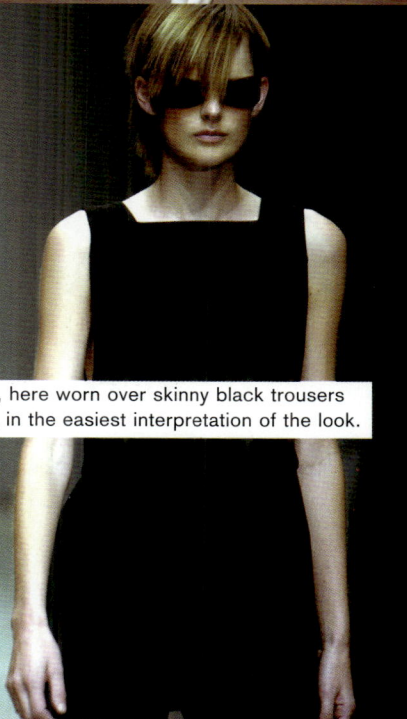

JUNYA WATANABE An army of beautiful alien school-girls has landed to show us all how to dress.

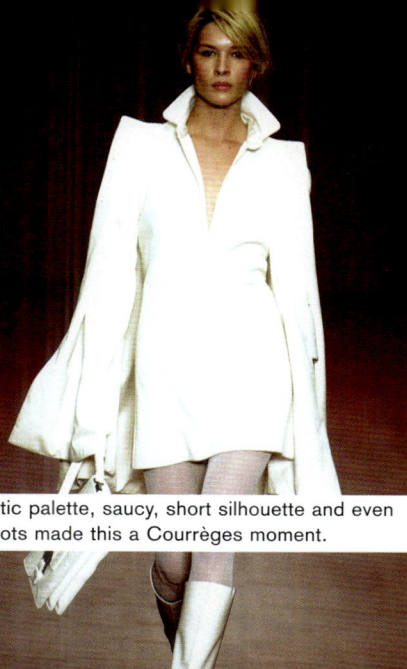

PRADA The minidress, here worn over skinny black trousers cut in the same fabric, in the easiest interpretation of the look.

FENDI Devon Aoki wins the Barbarella Award, 2001 in her silver minidress and go-go boots, courtesy of Monsieur Karl Lagerfeld.

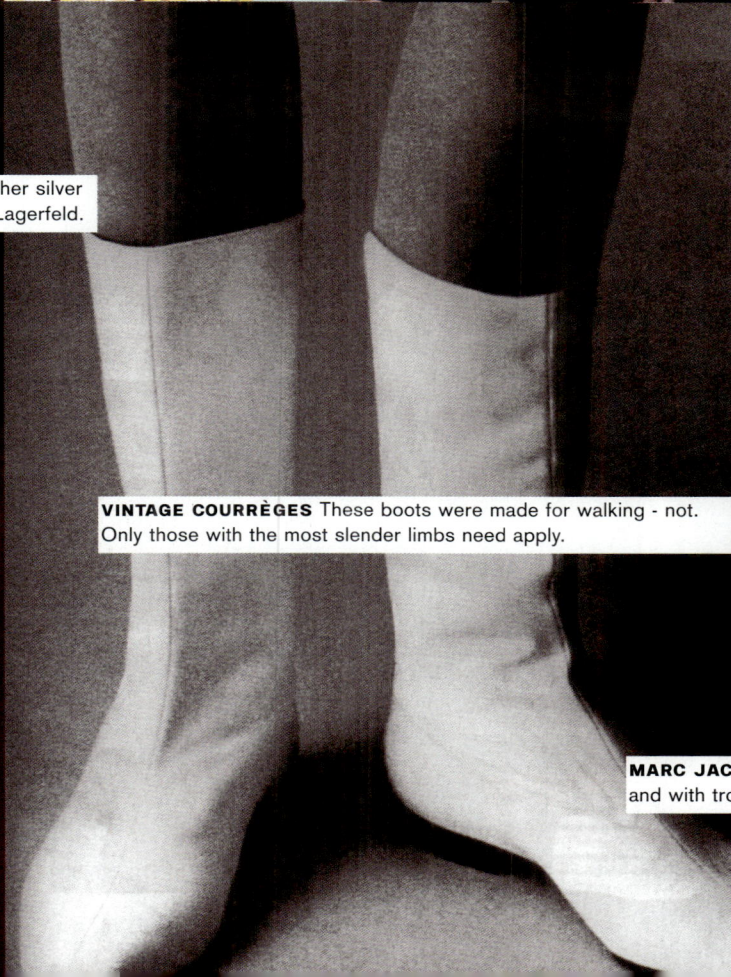

VINTAGE COURRÈGES These boots were made for walking - not. Only those with the most slender limbs need apply.

MARC JACOBS The '60s minidress printed with geometric shapes and with trompe l'oeil collar and waist.

burden of being cool than is usual for designer fashion.

Fendi is a label that has been deemed more cool than is strictly necessary for the past few seasons - it is still essentially a fur house but waiting lists for clothes and, in particular, accessories have seldom been so lengthy. This season, though, Lagerfeld relaxed his fashionable sang-froid a little and, with Watanabe, harked back to the glory days of the Courrèges archive. Sticking to the monochromatic palette so favoured by the era - white for the future, black and white for op art, was the, in retrospect, hugely over-simplified thinking of the time - Lagerfeld sent out leather trousers and cheeky mini-dresses with geometric cut-outs revealing circular flashes of skin. A little too close to the original? Perhaps. Devon Aoki, taking pride of place in the only silver version wins the Barbarella Award, 2001, however.

More Courrèges in Milan, where Miuccia Prada lent the look a bookish severity and the slightly off colour palette that has become one of her hallmarks. In true '60s style, mini coats and dresses had empire lines or dropped waists; and La Prada also came up with a solution for women who would rather not cram their legs into black opaque tights come the autumn. The mini dress - this time in black - worn over skinny black trousers cut in the same fabric is perhaps the most easy and modern interpretation of the trend. Further afield in New York, Calvin Klein and Marc Jacobs both revisited the '60s - Jacobs' interpretation was crisp and cute, printed with geometric shapes, embellished with oversized buttons and with trompe l'oeil collars and cuffs. But it was Anna Sui who went for the most literal interpretation - her models could have stepped straight out of the King's Road in its heyday and looked too much like a direct blast from fashion's past for comfort.

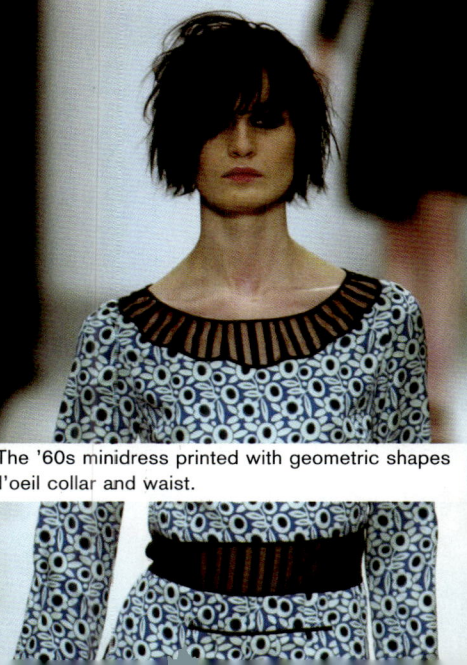

LITTLE GIRL LOST

If the '60s were all about a naive simplicity, a girlish but still ultimately rigorous silhouette and the ability to wear your youth on your sleeve and with pride, the '70s transformed this - via acres of flouncy, floaty fabric, into something rather less impressive. With this in mind, if there is one item of clothing in the fashion lexicon that brings out the blue-rinsed censor in this particular reviewer it is the baby doll dress. This utterly bizarre item of clothing first appeared, of course, in the decade that style forgot - think little girls' nighties in nylon fabrics and all the shades of pink, worn by precocious young Lolitas who wandered too close to a naked flame.

In the early '90s, Courtney Love put some attitude into the look, wearing it torn and tattered with a lop-sided tiara and hair that looked like it hadn't seen a brush for, well, for nigh on a decade. Her highly idiosyncratic style was picked up on by London street culture and was worn in clubs with a hefty dose of irony, alongside tiny t-shirts printed with "I'm cute", "fancy a snog" and other such saucy - and, frankly, nauseating - slogans. It seemed like the height of fashion at the time, I know.

Today, however, we really ought to know better but that hasn't stopped everyone from Tom Ford at Gucci, to Chanel and Lawrence Steele re-inventing the look. This begs the question: is it really okay for a grown woman to dress like a child? And the answer, according to the world's most fêted fashion designers, seems to be that, for the time being at least, it is. Even Comme des Garçons did a babydoll - just the one, admittedly, and styled almost insanely enough to make it look cool. And so did Helmut Lang, who, with this one rash move, very nearly toppled from his perch as a personal fashion hero for his sins. He was only saved by dropping his empire line to a marginally acceptable level, and giving his ivory sweet nothing of chiffon thick silk/satin shoulder straps.

He'll be relieved to hear of his ultimate reinstatement, I'm sure.

ALICE The object of Lewis Carroll's fevered, and none too healthy, imagination cropped up on catwalks the world over.

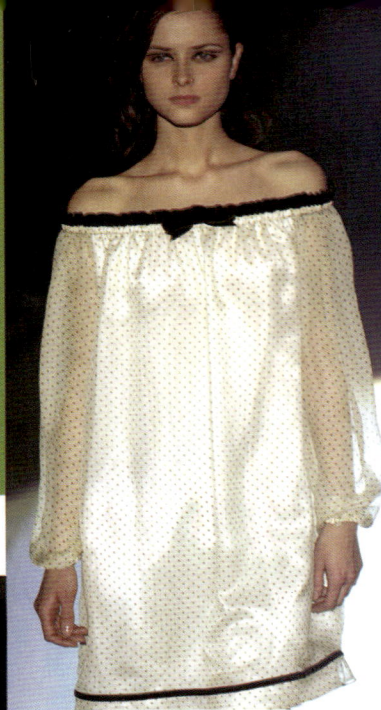

MIU MIU Grazing the ankle, this chiffon sweet nothing is pure Ossie Clark/Celia Birtwell.

LAWRENCE STEELE The baby doll dress begs the question: is it really alright for a grown woman to dress like a child.

CHANEL Every modern-day Alice needs a nanny - the Sound Of Music cape makes a comeback.

HELMUT LANG An unusually girlie moment courtesy of an unusually cool designer - he is forgiven such fashion frippery, of course.

SOUND OF MUSIC Julie Andrews and the Von Trapp's, the hills will be alive with the sound of capes flapping come autumn.

Maria kicks the habit.

ALICE: ILLUSTRATION: SIR JOHN TENNIEL COURTESY OF MACMILLAN & CO LTD. SOUND UP MUSIC: COURTESY OF MOVIESTORE. COURTNEY LOVE: SEATTLE 1994 THANKS TO JUERGEN TELLER

Elsewhere evidence of such saccharine sweet fashion frippery came with the revisitation of Wonderland - originally a Victorian creation, incidentally - and Alice its principal inhabitant who took centre stage. At Tanya Sarne's Ghost label - now presided over by Amy Roberts, formerly of the Galliano stable - Alice came in the form of sexy bias cut, asymmetric black georgette dresses emblazoned with "shrunk" or "eat me". At Miu Miu, meanwhile, the silhouette more than nodded to the object of Lewis Carroll's fevered and, it has to be said, none too healthy imagination: all frothy empire-line dresses with skirts too full to be entirely dignified and pretty puffed sleeves, accessorised with sensible t-bar shoes. It is testimony to the ultimately very subtle nature of fashion that, worn short, these did little for even the world's most beautiful women. Grazing the ankle, however, basically the same dresses looked more Ossie Clark/Celia Birtwell than bed-time story. Funny how the '70s, seen through the eyes of the '30s, never seem quite so bad.

Finally, as we all know, every modern day Alice is quite lost without a nanny and in this, too, the collections didn't disappoint. Miu Miu's big sister, Prada, was more than happy to oblige with an aesthetic severe enough in parts to come directly from the über-nanny's very own wardrobe. This is particularly true of the autumn/winter Prada cape - a Julie Andrews stalwart, and a major trend for autumn/winter elsewhere, too, for that matter. At Chanel it was lovely in pale tweed.

GHOST Wonderland lives and breathes on the London catwalk.

PRADA It's a cape Von Trapp, and you've been caught.

COMME DES GARÇONS The baby doll styled almost insanely enough to make the fashion grade.

COURTNEY LOVE A woman hard enough to make even the baby doll dress look cool - this is impressive.

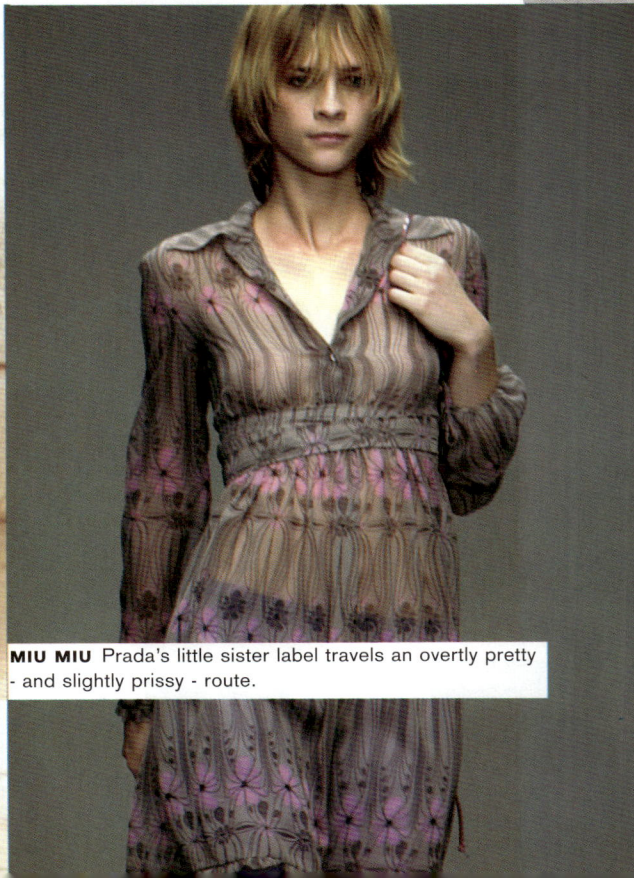

MIU MIU Prada's little sister label travels an overtly pretty - and slightly prissy - route.

GUCCI And another one - enough, already.

GENDER BENDING

It's bizarre to think that, at the beginning of the 20th century, a woman risked being arrested for taking the liberty of wearing trousers. A few brave souls - notably Sarah Bernhardt - wore them as early as the late 19th century but it was, clearly, not to be recommended. It was Coco Chanel, who first made trousers acceptable for the fairer sex, in the form of "yachting pants" for wear at the beach - to save women the indignity of their skirts blowing up in the breeze, perhaps? During the '50s, the young and fashionable pushed the boat out in pedalpushers - a decidedly girlish variation on the theme. It wasn't really until the '60s and the emergence of unisex fashion that trousers for women really came into their own.

The world has Yves Saint Laurent to thank for the woman's trouser suit. His by now hugely famous Le Smoking was first sent out in '66 and, even as late as that, caused an uproar. This is hardly surprising. Women's eveningwear, up until that time, was, for the most part, a distinctly frilly affair. Overnight girls had a very sleek and chic alternative and one that endures to this day.

Almost 40 years on, if women prefer not to dress in an overtly feminine way - and indeed, if men feel the need to wear skirts - they will always have the option of androgyny to turn to and no one will bat an eyelid. Throughout the late '70s and '80s, the man's trouser suit was the thinking woman's way to dress. Giorgio Armani's unstructured tailoring in neutral colours was worn to prove just how serious women really were. Today, the trouser suit, and all other dress codes borrowed from men, for that matter, are just some of the many ways to assert a notion of femininity that is, happily, no longer fixed.

This season, in particular, the trouser suit came as a highly welcome alternative to ultra-feminine flounces, and in many different guises. Most notable was the collection of Martin Margiela. For two years now, Maison Martin Margiela has scaled up his clothes for women to a "fictive men's Italian size 78" - as you do. "We have over many seasons sought to explore a contrast in

Walk like a man...

VINTAGE YVES SAINT LAURENT When the designer first sent out the Le Smoking in 1966 he revolutionised the way women dress.

VINTAGE CHANEL Madame Chanel's "yachting pants" were the first ever designer trousers deemed acceptable for women.

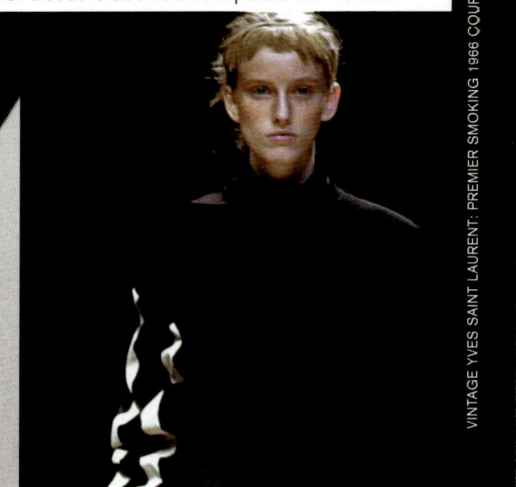

YOHJI YAMAMOTO The trouser suit deconstructed then reconstructed with sportswear references and an adidas stripe.

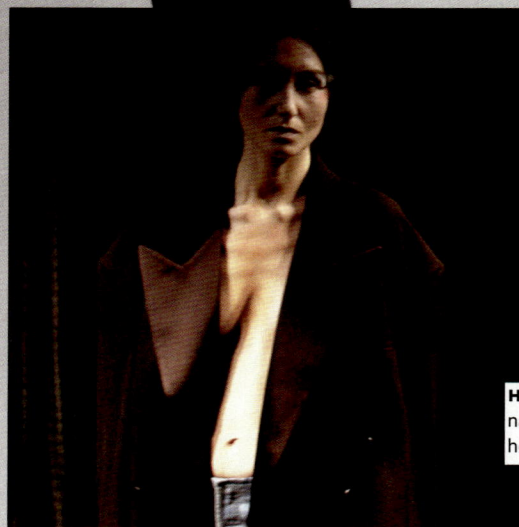

MARTIN MARGIELA Men's jackets sized up to "a fictive men's Italian size 78" explores a contrast in proportion.

HELMUT LANG A heavy black trouser suit with narrow shoulders and skinny pants shows just how relaxed a tailored two-piece can be.

VINTAGE YVES SAINT LAURENT: PREMIER SMOKING 1966 COURTESY OF YSL ARCHIVE. VINTAGE CHANEL: MADEMOISELLE CHANEL CIRCA 1930 PHOTOGRAPHY DR

MARLENE DIETRICH: PHOTOGRAPHY WILLIAM WALLING JNR COURTESY OF THE KOBAL COLLECTION. BIANCA JAGGER: COURTESY OF SIPA PRESS \ REX FEATURES

proportion between garments and those who wear them," states the house. "Proposing men's garments - as against women's garments with a masculine feel - has been a recurring theme of our collection for many years. These garments maintain all the aspects considered part and parcel of mens-wear: internal pockets, buttoning and the various linings used for men's jackets, fabric weights and types. It has always been interesting for us to explore the juxtaposition of men's garments with those of a more feminine allure." With this in mind, as well as oversized men's jackets that have the happy effect of making a woman appear small - if never cutely so - in her clothes, new to the Margiela fold this season were men's Victorian housecoats in rich colours and fabrics, contrasted by very feminine fringed dresses worn beneath.

At Givenchy, Alexander McQueen, similarly played on the juxtaposition between masculine and feminine to rather lovely effect. For his swan-song show for the house - shown in the salon and to only 80 people - the designer kept things simpler than he has done and the collection looked strong for it. Narrow, masculine trouser suits were given a feminine twist worn with sweeping open skirts; the masculine nature of men's shirting, meanwhile, was subvert-ed, cut as it was, into full, tiered skirts. As far as the modern trouser suit is concerned, Helmut Lang reigns supreme - and this time round was no exception. A heavy black satin trouser suit for women - it is by now a classic in his menswear archive - with slightly sloping shoulders

and wickedly narrow pants, showed just how cool, relaxed even, a tailored two-piece can be. Tuxedo dresses at Lang and McQueen played on a similar masculine meets feminine feel.

In Paris, Yohji Yamamoto this time, as always, gave good suit. In a collection that owed its inspiration to sportswear, executed with the attention to detail of haute couture, roomy hoods, cape-shoulders, wide-legged trousers and, new this season, Yohji trainers - all embellished with the adidas stripe made a hugely complex, but still very relaxed, silhouette more coolly downbeat still. Balenciaga's trouser suit came tight-fitting - sexy but brilliantly severe. The narrow Balenciaga trouser has a cult following, and for good reason. John Galliano travelled a more eclectic route for his collection for Christian Dior: loud blazers went from Irish tinker to Cuban gangster in flavour. Young British designer, Marcus Constable, mean-while, gave the city gent a feminine overhaul with striped men's shirting, cut on the bias, and sexed up, high-waisted masculine tailoring ■

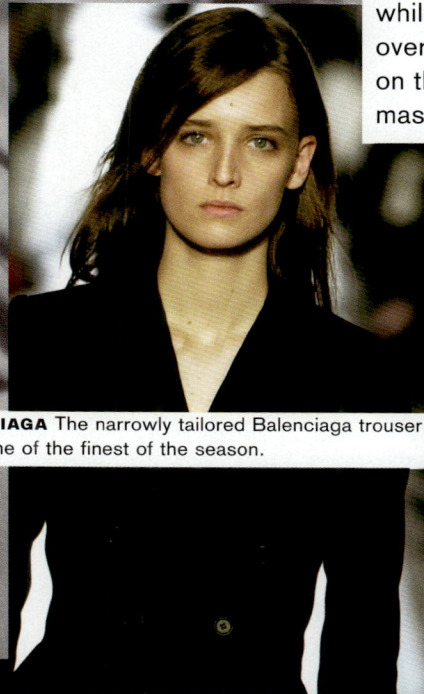

MARLENE DIETRICH Man drag at its most exquisitely lovely - and worn long ago enough to cause sartorial shock-waves.

BALENCIAGA The narrowly tailored Balenciaga trouser suit is one of the finest of the season.

MARTIN MARGIELA The men's Victorian housecoat in rich colours and textures makes a welcome addition to the designer's stable.

BIANCA JAGGER An icon in a white trouser suit - this image continues to inspire fashion shoots to this day.

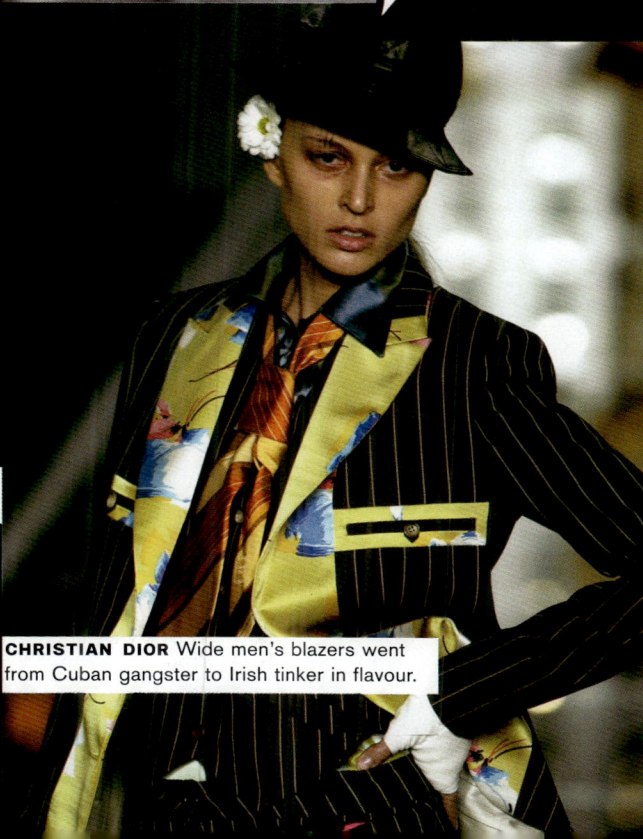

CHRISTIAN DIOR Wide men's blazers went from Cuban gangster to Irish tinker in flavour.

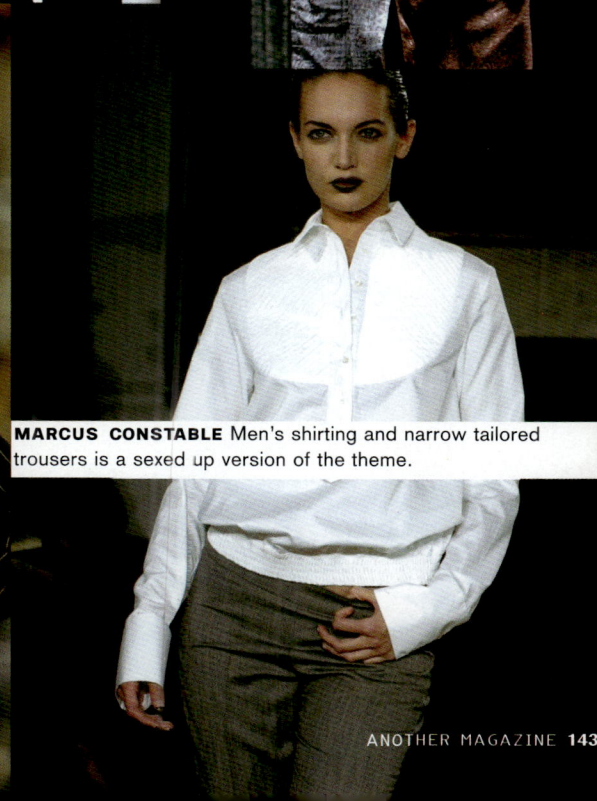

MARCUS CONSTABLE Men's shirting and narrow tailored trousers is a sexed up version of the theme.

VERSACE

VERSACE

VERSACE

THE COLLECTIONS:
Celebrate this season in sartorial splendor.

"The only PERFORMANCE that really really makes it is the one that achieves madness."

TURNER IN NICOLAS ROEG AND DONALD CAMMELL'S *PERFORMANCE*

PHOTOGRAPHY **PHIL POYNTER**
STYLING WOMENSWEAR **KATY ENGLAND**
STYLING MENSWEAR **TABITHA SIMMONS**
HAIR **MALCOLM EDWARDS** AT **UNTITLED*** USING **L'OREAL**
MAKE-UP **VAL GARLAND** AT **UNTITLED*** USING **CALVIN KLEIN COSMETICS**
PRODUCTION **NICK** AT **CLM** AND **MUNGO MACLAGAN**
STREET CASTING **OTIS** AND **JAMES** AT **JM CASTING**
STYLING ASSISTANCE AND FASHION COORDINATION **SARA BURN**
LOCATION SCOUT **BELAL ASHRAF**
RETOUCHING **THE SHOEMAKERS ELVES**
PROCESSING **GOLDENSHOTS**
LIGHTING AND EQUIPMENT **DIRECT LIGHTING**
PHOTOGRAPHIC ASSISTANTS **DAN ANNETT, BEN RICHARDSON** AND **BELAL ASHRAF**
HAIR ASSISTANCE **SELENA MIDDLETON, MAARIT NIEMELA,**
WILLIAM KONG, PAUL HANLON AND **MATT RAINE**
MAKE-UP ASSISTANCE **PETROHILOS** AND **NATSKA**
BOOKINGS **JOHANNA METHUSALEMSDOTTIR**

ALWAYS FROM LEFT TO RIGHT:
JANE PEACHY, PHILLIPA, SARA, JULIET FORESTER AT MODELS 1, KAREN PEACHY,
MARTHA, CHARLIE, PAM PHILLIPS AT UGLY AND MARIANNA AT STORM.
PEDRO AND RICARDO GUEDES AT SO DAM TUFF WEAR PANTS BY **SPEEDO**;
BOXING BOOTS BY **LONSDALE**. **CHANEL**

VALENTINE (FRONT) AT VIVA, ALISTAIR COLDREY AT SELECT, SYLVIA AT NEXT, SCOTT TEMPLE AND DOMINIC BRIDER AT SELECT, MELODY AT STORM, PAW AT SELECT AND RICHARD CLOUSTON.

COMME DES GARÇONS

VERSACE ALL GIRLS WEAR **VERSACE**. BLACK PATENT LEATHER BOOTS BY **CHRISTIAN LOUBOUTIN**.

DOLCE&GABBANA BILL GENTLE AT SELECT, EVA PADBERG AT MODELS 1, PATRICK MOSSON, MELANIE, MATTHEW MOLYNEUX, ANNA L AT SELECT AND BOPPO.

ANA PAULA AT NEXT, JOANNE WALPOLE AT MODELS 1, DUNCAN HILL, STINE AT BOOKINGS, HOBI AT STORM, IRENE AT MODELS 1, KOJI , THOMAS BLAK
AT OXYGEN, RICHARD, KATYA AND RUSSELL COOTE AT SELECT, JON JO, HENRIK UBSTOV, RAMONA, SEAN REVERON AT TAKE 2 AND CECILIA.
AMANDA JOHNSON (FRONT) AT TAKE 2. THOMAS AND JON JO WEAR SHOES BY **CONVERSE**; SEAN WEARS SHOES BY **TRICKERS**.

GIVENCHY

JASJA BOELHOUWER (STANDING)
WEARS **CAROL CHRISTIAN
POELL**, SPARKLE MOORE
WEARS RED NIGHTWEAR,
VINTAGE STOCKINGS AND
SHOES ALL FROM THE GIRL
CAN'T HELP IT.

CHRISTIAN LACROIX   MALIN AT NEXT AND JAN DE VILLENEUVE AT MODELS 1 WEAR **CHRISTIAN LACROIX**, TIGHTS BY **FOGAL**, GLIN CALLINGHAM (CENTRE) WEARS **HELMUT LANG**.

DIOR SHOJI, MARIA, WILLIAM, ZHANNA AT STORM, JON NG AT TAKE 2, ANGIE R AT STORM, AND JOSEPH ALL WEAR **DIOR HOMME** BY HEDI SLIMANE, SERENE (CENTRE) AT IMG LONDON WEARS BLUE GOWN AND SHORTS BY **CHRISTIAN DIOR**, BRA BY **AGENT PROVOCATEUR**, BLACK PATENT LEATHER BOOTS BY **FREELANCE SHOES**.

TIM CLIFFTON GREEN, LAURENCE AND BABE, AZHAR AT OXYGEN,
CARLTON AND MATTHEW BRYNJOLFSSON ALL WEAR **RAF SIMONS**;
CYNTHIA UDRIOT AT MAJOR NY (FRONT) WEARS
BALENCIAGA "LE DIX".

MARTIN MARGIELA AMANDA MOORE AT NEXT, JACEY AT SELECT AND WILD CAT WILL WEAR **MARTIN MARGIELA**. AMANDA WEARS KNICKERS FROM **MARKS & SPENCER**.

CHANEL SHOT AT STRINGFELLOWS 16-19 UPPER SAINT MARTINS LANE COVENT GARDEN WC2H 9EF. (+44) 20 7240 5534

GUCCI AND **DOLCE & GABBANA** SHOT AT YE OLD AXE 69 HACKNEY ROAD E2. (+44) 20 7729 5137. WITH THANKS TO TOM MELODY.

PRADA SHOT AT CRASH NIGHTCLUB 66 GODING STREET SE11. (+44) 020 7820 1500. WITH THANKS TO BRIE.

COMME DES GARÇONS SHOT AT AGENT PROVOCATEUR WITH THANKS TO SERENA REES AND JOSEPH CORRÉ. (+44) 20 7235 0229 WWW.AGENTPROVOCATEUR.COM

JEAN PAUL GAULTIER WITH THANKS TO ANDY LINK (WWW.NORTHLAND.CO.UK) FOR USE OF HIS BOUDCIR AND PLAYROOM.

CHRISTIAN LACROIX SHOT AT ZOO BAR 13-17 BEAR STREET LEICESTER SQUARE WC2. (+44) 20 7839 4188. WITH THANKS TO CHRISTOPHER MARTIN.

CHRISTIAN DIOR SHOT AT METROPOLIS THE PLEASURE LOUNGE, 234 CAMBRIDGE HEATH ROAD LONDON E2 9NN. (+44) 20 8980 2917. WITH THANKS TO STEVE.

CONCEPT AND ART DIRECTION **STELLA McCARTNEY**
PHOTOGRAPHY **MATTHIAS VRIENS** AT **WALTER SCHUPFER**
MAKE-UP **FERIDE USLU** AT **FRAME**
HAIR **ROLANDO BEAUCHAMP** FOR **BUMBLE & BUMBLE**
MANICURIST **BERNADETTE THOMPSON** AT **ZANE AGENCY**
PHOTOGRAPHIC ASSISTANTS **JASON WILLS, SAM BUFFA**
AND **PETER BURGSTALLER**
MAKE-UP ASSISTANT **MIZU**
RETOUCHING **RAPHAEL DAHAN** AT **4TH-FLOOR NY**
PRODUCTION **TERESA FARRELL** AT **WALTER SCHUPFER**
PROCESSING **SMALL DARK ROOM**
THANKS TO **MILK STUDIOS NY**

BLACK & WHITE:
A Hollywood Classic

Stella McCartney stepped out of the design studio to guest art direct the centrefold exclusively for this issue of Another Magazine. Featuring her friends, actress Kate Hudson and husband, musician Chris Robinson, Stella McCartney has created the ultimate pin-up statement. Her vision of male and female sexuality for this season is romantic, not too revealing and ultimately sexy. She shows that friendships and a loving relationship are the strongest link. Stella McCartney will be showing her debut collection under her own name this season, during Paris Fashion Week.

Oscar nominated actress **Kate Hudson** is set to appear in two forthcoming films this year: Four Feathers by Shekhar Kapur, the director of Elizabeth, and How To Loose A Guy In 10 Days by Mike Newell.

Chris Robinson, lead singer of The Black Crowes, has just
completed a world tour promoting his latest album, Lions.

ICEBERG

ICEBERG

ICEBERG

DESIRE

You know what you like.
You wear what you want.
Fashion, now, more than ever, is a
matter of personal choice.
It's about originality, individuality,
and freedom. Let your emotions dictate
the adventure and fashion
will follow your lead.

PHOTOGRAPHY **MARIO SORRENTI**
STYLING **CAMILLA NICKERSON**
HAIR **RECINE**
MAKE-UP **FRANK B** AT THE WALL GROUP
MODELS **AN OOST** AT FORD MODELS, **LOLA
MONTES SCHNABEL, VITO MARIA SCHNABEL,
ANATOL, LUCIE DE LA FALAISE** AT WOMEN
MODEL MANAGEMENT, **ALMA CONTINANZI,
JOE TORCZON, PAUL BREE, NATHANAEL
ALBRIGHT, WILL ALBRIGHT, DAVID MOBLEY**
AND **JONATHAN DALY**
PHOTOGRAPHIC ASSISTANTS **LARS BEAULIEU,
DAVID SCHECTER** AND **KENNY JOSSICK**
STYLING ASSISTANT **AVENA GALLAGHER**
PRODUCTION **STEVE SUTTON** AT SORRENTI & SUTTON
PROPS **PHILIP HAEMMERLE**
THANKS TO **JOHN** AND **JOAN DALY** FOR THE USE OF
THEIR HOUSE

THE CAZZO'S (FROM LEFT) GUITARIST WEARS
MARC JACOBS MEN TROUSERS, ZIP-UP JACKET
MODELS OWN, DRUMMER WEARS DENIM
JEANS BY **CALVIN KLEIN JEANS**, BASS PLAYER
WEARS BLACK HOODED SWEATSHIRT BY
STÜSSY AND JEANS BY **LEVI'S**.

ANATOL WEARS BLACK T-SHIRT BY **ORFI**;
ALL OTHER CLOTHES MODELS OWN.

JOE WEARS WETSUIT BY **O'NEILL**; PAUL WEARS
WETSUIT BY **QUIKSILVER**; NATHANAEL, WILL AND
DAVID WEAR WETSUITS BY **LIDO SURF COMPANY**;
JONATHAN WEARS WETSUIT BY **QUIKSILVER**.

LUCIE WEARS VELVET BABY DOLL DRESS BY **GUCCI**,
ALMA WEARS BLACK SUIT BY **ANTEPRIMA**.

SHOT AT **FRED LEIGHTON RARE COLLECTIBLE JEWELS**
773 MADISON AVE, NEW YORK, NY 10012. (+212) 288 1872

MARIO WEARS MAROON BOMBER JACKET
WITH WOOL COAT TAILS BY **RAF SIMONS**.

TWO

PHOTOGRAPHY TERRY RICHARDSON
STYLING SABINA SCHREDER
GROOMING DENIS LANNI FOR BUMBLE & BUMBLE AT FRAME
CASTING BARBARA PFISTER
FILM AND PRINT PROCESSING RIAZ AT C LAB NY
PHOTOGRAPHIC ASSISTANT SETH GOLDFARB
STYLING ASSISTANT RENATA ABBADE
MODELS CARL AND CARLOS
SPECIAL THANKS TO PASCAL DANGIN AT BOX LTD NY

CARL (ON FLOOR) WEARS CHECKED BUTTON DOWN SHIRT BY **VIVIENNE WESTWOOD MAN**; JEANS BY **GUCCI**; SOCKS BY **POLO RALPH LAUREN**,
CARLOS (ON CHAIR) WEARS DENIM TUXEDO SUIT BY **GIANFRANCO FERRE**; WHITE BUTTON DOWN SHIRT BY **DONNA KARAN**.

CARL WEARS SWEATER BY **PAUL SMITH**; TROUSERS BY **HELMUT LANG**; STRIPED SHIRT BY **NINA RICCI MEN**; SILK SCARF BY **HERMÈS**, CARLOS WEARS NAVY SUIT AND WHITE SILK SHIRT BY **GIANFRANCO FERRE**.

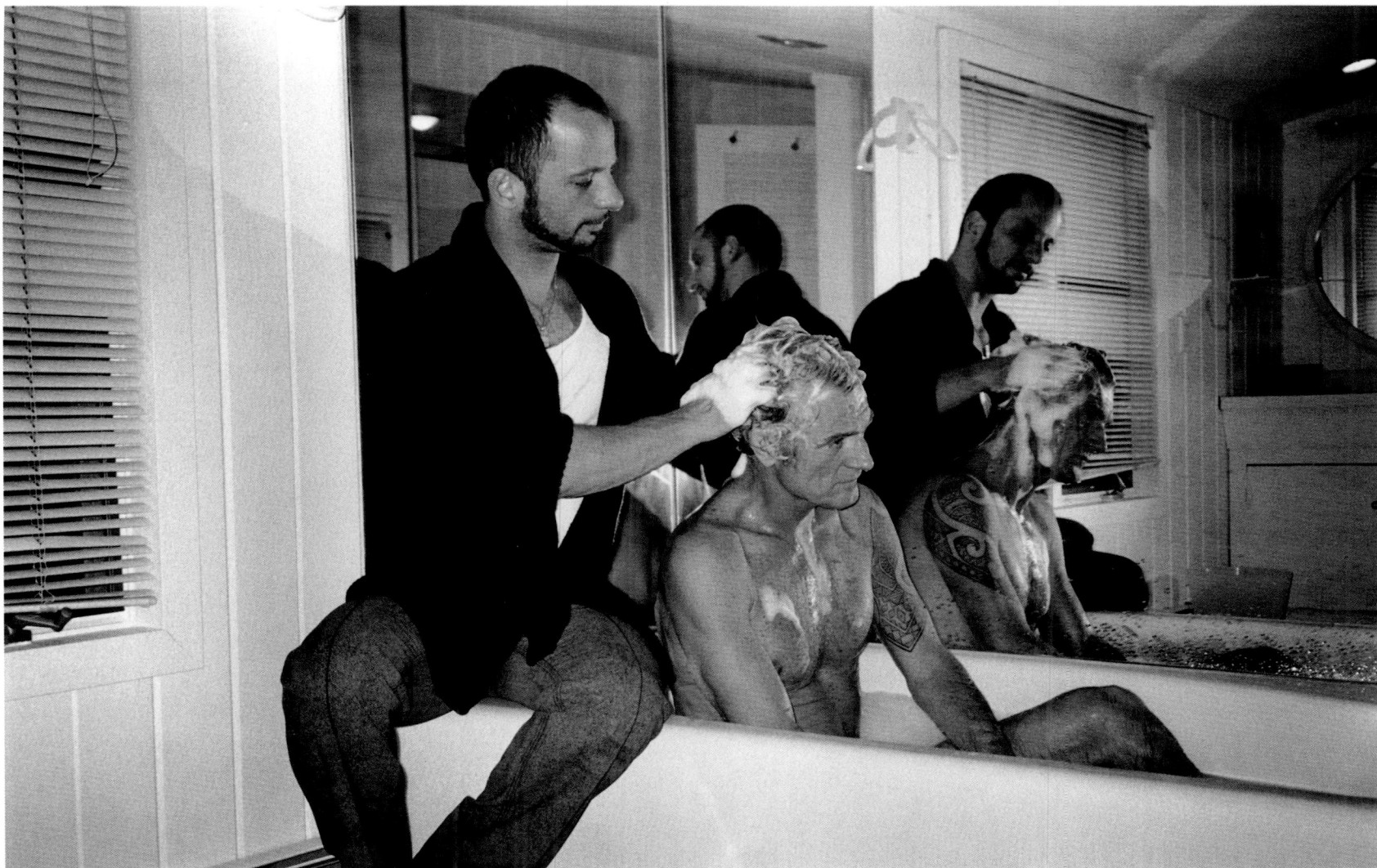

CARLOS WEARS KNIT ROBE BY **GUCCI**; WOOL TROUSERS BY **COSTUME NATIONAL**; TANK TOP BY **CALVIN KLEIN**.

CARLOS WEARS SUIT BY **MARTIN MARGIELA**; WHITE SCARF BY **JIL SANDER**; TANK TOP BY **CALVIN KLEIN**; BOOTS BY **CAROL CHRISTIAN POELL**; NECKLACE MODELS OWN,
CARL WEARS KNITTED CREAM SWEATER BY **MARTIN MARGIELA**; STRIPED SHIRT BY **LOUIS VUITTON**; TROUSERS BY **MARC JACOBS MEN**; BOOTS BY **PAUL SMITH**.

CARLOS WEARS WHITE COTTON PIQUÈ SHIRT BY **VALENTINO**.

CARL WEARS COTTON JACKET BY **MARC JACOBS MEN**; STRIPED SHIRT **EMANUEL UNGARO**; CORDUROY PANTS BY **TRUSSARDI**; LEATHER BELT BY **HERMÈS**, CARLOS WEARS GREY WOOL SWEATER VEST BY **CAROL CHRISTIAN POELL**; STRIPED SHIRT BY **COSTUME NATIONAL**; WOOL PANTS BY **TRUSSARDI**; SHOES **Y'S FOR MEN** BY **YOHJI YAMAMOTO**; SCARF STYLIST'S OWN.

CARLOS WEARS CORDUROY JACKET BY **PAUL SMITH**; TURTLENECK BY **DONNA KARAN**, CARL WEARS SWEATER BY **LOUIS VUITTON**; STRIPED SHIRT BY **PAUL SMITH**; SILK SCARF BY **HERMÈS**.

CARLOS WEARS BOXERS BY **CALVIN KLEIN**, CARL WEARS WHITE SHIRT AND CARDIGAN BY **LOUIS VUITTON**.

CARL WEARS WOOL COAT BY **YOHJI YAMAMOTO**; KNITTED SCARF BY **VIVIENNE WESTWOOD MAN**, CARLOS WEARS JACKET AND TURTLENECK BY **LOUIS VUITTON**; TROUSERS BY **YOHJI YAMAMOTO**.

three

PHOTOGRAPHY **NICK KNIGHT**
STYLING **KATY ENGLAND**
HAIR **SAM MCKNIGHT** AT **PREMIER**
MAKE-UP **VAL GARLAND** AT **UNTITLED*** USING **CALVIN KLEIN COSMETICS**
NAIL TECHNICIAN **NATALIE COLLINS** FOR **AMALGAMATED TALENT**
SCANNING **IDEA DIGITAL IMAGING**
THANKS TO **METRO IMAGING LTD** AND **LAYTON NORTHCLIFFE CASTING**
MODELS **ZORA STAR** AT **TAKE 2** AND **OLIVIER ROBERT**
PHOTOGRAPHIC ASSISTANTS **BEN DUNBAR-BRUNTON, NAOMI WALKER,**
DOMINIC COOPER
STYLING ASSISTANT **SARA BURN**
LOCATION FINDER **WWW.COMPASSLOCATIONS.COM**

TOM WEARS TROUSERS BY **VERSACE**; TOP BY **COSTUME NATIONAL**; BLACK CUMBERBAND BY **HELMUT LANG**; EMBROIDERED CUMBERBAND BY **MICHAEL AND HUSH**; GOLD CHAIN BRACELET AND OLD COIN BRACELET BY **MENDED VEIL**.

PHOTOGRAPHY **GREG KADEL** STYLING **TABITHA SIMMONS**
HAIR **SHARON DOWSETT** FOR **MAC COSMETICS** MAKE-UP **MANDY LYONS** FOR **BUMBLE AND BUMBLE** STYLING ASSISTANTS **MIA BAKER**
MODELS **RIE RASMUSSEN** AT **KARIN NY** AND **TOM ABBOT** AT **IMG**
SPECIAL THANKS TO **STEVE** AT **IMPACT DIGITAL**, **TODD ASHLEY**, **CHRISTIAN CAMARGO**, **OMEE DELING** AND **GYPSY** AT **FAST ASHLEY STUDIOS**

PHOTOGRAPHY RICHARD BURBRIDGE
STYLING SABINA SCHREDER
MAKE-UP LENA KORO AT TIFFANY WHITFORD
PHOTOGRAPHIC ASSISTANTS STEFAN KOCHS,
RICHARD LEE AND BOOKER
STYLING ASSISTANTS RENATA ABBADE
AND AMI SIOUX
CASTING JENNIFER BAPTISTA
MODELS MEGAN SHOEMAKER AT COMPANY
MANAGEMENT, MARIE EVE NADEAU AT DNA,
SEAN HUGHES AT IMG NY, KELLY SAWYER AT
KARIN NY, TOMAS HUSA AND VICTORIA STOKES
AT NEW YORK MODEL, CONSUELO ADLER AT
WILHELMINA
THANKS TO MILK STUDIOS NY

15

ALWAYS FROM LEFT TO RIGHT:
PAGE 218
MEGAN WEARS JACKET (CUT IN HALF) VINTAGE YVES
SAINT LAURENT; PULLOVER (ON SHOULDER) AND SHIRT
SKIRT BY MIGUEL ADROVER; ROPE BELT BY JILL
STUART, MARIE EVE WEARS NAVY AND WHITE
STRIPED SHIRT BY CALVIN KLEIN JEANS; GREEN TEA
TULLE TOP BY AS FOUR; LEATHER AND CHAIN BROOCH
FROM KENI VALENTI; BLACK SKIRT BELT BY JILL
STUART, KELLY WEARS STRIPED SHIRT BY TOMMY
HILFIGER; VEST SHIRT AND TROUSERS BY MIGUEL
ADROVER; CREAM RUFFLES FROM K TRIMMING;
VINTAGE BROOCH PAINTED WHITE, CONSUELO WEARS
PRINTED SHIRT BY WILLIAM REID; DRESS BY MIGUEL
ADROVER; METAL TOP BY PLEIN SUD; TUXEDO BELT
BY VIVIENNE WESTWOOD, VICTORIA WEARS BLUE
STRIPED SHIRT BY RALPH LAUREN; WHITE CORSET
BY VIVIENNE WESTWOOD; BELT BY CAROL
CHRISTIAN POELL; VINTAGE TROUSERS BY YOHJI
YAMAMOTO FROM KENI VALENTI.

PAGE 220
MEGAN WEARS BLACK SILK JERSEY DRESS BY
NARCISO RODRIGUEZ; OFF WHITE COTTON SHIRT BY
IMITATION OF CHRIST; AND GREY TULLE POM POM
CIRCLE BAG BY AS FOUR.

PAGE 222
TOMAS WEARS BOOT PRINT HALF JACKET STYLISTS
OWN; BLACK LEATHER JACKET WITH STARS BY
VERSUS; CROTCHLESS TROUSERS BY CAROL
CHRISTIAN POELL, MARIE EVE WEARS CHECKED
BUTTON DOWN SHIRT BY RALPH LAUREN; WHITE
TURTLENECK BY MARC BY MARC JACOBS; VINTAGE
NYLON SWEATPANTS BY NIKE; CHARCOAL STRETCH
CAGE VEST BY HELMUT LANG; SEQUIN GLOVE BY
CAROL CHRISTIAN POELL, CONSUELO WEARS
GREY TROUSERS BY MARTIN MARGIELA; VINTAGE
GREY STRIPED SHIRT BY CHRISTIAN DIOR; GREEN
T-SHIRT WITH BLACK SPLOTCHES BY FAKE GENIUS;
SPOON NECKLACE BY JODY BUSBY; KNIT JACKET BY
VIVIENNE WESTWOOD; GREY STRIPED VEST BY
HELMUT LANG.

PAGE 224
SEAN WEARS BLACK AND WHITE PINSTRIPE SUIT BY **ISSEY MIYAKE MEN**; STRIPED SHIRT (CUT IN HALF) BY **MARC JACOBS MEN**; VINTAGE T-SHIRT; WHITE ELASTIC CORD BELT BY **CAROL CHRISTIAN POELL**, CONSUELO WEARS BLACK COMPRESSED T-SHIRT BY **MARTIN MARGIELA**; WHITE LEATHER COLLAR-BRACES BY **CAROL CHRISTIAN POELL**; GREY TROUSERS BY **HELMUT LANG**, VICTORIA WEARS OFF WHITE SHIRT BY **UNITED BAMBOO**; LEATHER STRIPED VEST BY **PLEIN SUD**; HIGH WAIST SHORTS BY **CAROL CHRISTIAN POELL**, KELLY WEARS BLACK VELVET TOP BY **MARIA**; "FUCK LOVE" PRINT SILK BLOUSE BY **MATT MADE IN THE USA**; POLKA DOT GLOVES BY **MISSONI**; NECKLACE FROM CHELSEA FLEA MARKET, VINTAGE LACE COLLAR, TOMAS WEARS GREEN PLASTIC JACKET; GREEN SHIRT AND TROUSERS BY **ISSEY MIYAKE MEN**; DARK GREEN TURTLENECK BY **CAROL CHRISTIAN POELL**.

PAGE 226
TOMAS WEARS GREY BUTTON DOWN SHIRT BY **VIVIENNE WESTWOOD MAN**; WHITE SLEEVELESS SHIRT WITH LARGE DOTS BY **MATT MADE IN THE USA**; GREY BACKLESS WAISTCOAT BY **CAROL CHRISTIAN POELL**; JEANS BY **LEVI'S VINTAGE COLLECTION**; VINTAGE T-SHIRT, SEAN WEARS SILVER LUREX SHIRT BY **MISSONI**; JEANS BY **LEVI'S RED**; BLACK LEATHER SCARF BY **JILL STUART**; VINTAGE T-SHIRT AND JACKET.

PAGE 228
KELLY WEARS FUR HAIRCUT BY **EUGENIA KIM**; SILVER SEQUIN TOP BY **MARNI**; FEATHER SHOULDER REST BY **HELMUT LANG**, SEAN WEARS FEATHER PRINT SCARF AND GREEN AND WHITE PRINT SCARF BY **HERMÈS**; NECKLACE BY **JODY BUSBY**; FUR SCARF BY **JIL SANDER**.

228 ANOTHER MAGAZINE

JILSANDER

Soul Windows.

PHOTOGRAPHY **DAVID SIMS**
STYLING **KATY ENGLAND**
HAIR **GUIDO**
MAKE-UP **LINDA CANTELLO** FOR **LINDA CANTELLO COSMETICS**
MODELS **JULIE M** AT **BOSS, DOROTA** AT **DNA, EMILY HOPE** AT **SELECT,**
ELIANA WEIRICH, MARCELLE BITTAR AND **LUKA SYLWESTER** AT **SUPREME**
PHOTOGRAPHIC ASSISTANTS **LEE BROOMFIELD** AND **NIKKI SIMS**
STYLING ASSISTANT **ALANA GABBIN**
PRODUCTION **AMANDA HAAN**
RETOUCHING **SHOEMAKERS ELVES**
SHOT AT **MILK STUDIOS NY**

LUKA WEARS **PROTECTIVE MOISTURE CREAM**;
EYE COLOR WASH IN **RED SEA**; **LIP COLOR** IN **POPPY**;
LIP GLOSS IN **APRICOT GLAZE** AND **BROW GROOMER**
ALL BY **CALVIN KLEIN COSMETICS**.

EMILY WEARS TINTED MOISTURISER NO1.
AND LIPSUEDE BOTH BY LINDA CANTELLO.

ELIANA WEARS **LINDA CANTELLO FORGET FOUNDATION**.

MARCELLE WEARS **VITOLMINE RADIENCE ACTIVATOR**
AND **ROUGE BRILLIENT LIP GLOSS**
BOTH BY **CHRISTIAN DIOR**.

LUKA WEARS **HYDRATING SERUM**
AND **SHEILDING LIP CREAM SPF12**
BOTH BY **PRADA BEAUTY**.

JULIE M WEARS **DAYWEAR** PROTECTIVE **ANTI-OXIDANT LOTION** BY **ESTÉE LAUDER**.

DOROTA WEARS **VINEFITE ENERGISING MOISTURISER**;
BLUSH POMMETTE IN **ROSE CONDIDE** AND **LIP BRIO**
IN **COCO** ALL BY **LANCÔME**.

Another Document
Premiere Issue

LETTERS ... from 100 Years Ago

THE JOURNEY

To the editor of The View,

Sir, - A short while past, a young man came to visit me. He asked, 'What ought I to do to sleep peacefully at night?' 'Young man,' I replied, 'you are an atheist and a believer in naturalism. What has happened?' 'Devil take it! When I got home last night and opened my door someone took hold of my arm and shook me.' 'So there was someone in your room?' I countered. 'Why, no! I lit the candles and could not see anyone.' 'Young man,' I persisted, 'there is one whom we cannot see by the light of a candle.' 'What manner of being is he?' he asked. 'He is the unseen, young man. Have you taken sulphonal, potassium bromide, morphia?' 'I have tried them all,' he said. 'And the unseen won't decamp? Well, I am no doctor, nor am I a prophet; I am an old sinner, doing penance. I too have fought face to face with the Unseen, and I have at last regained the power of sleep and got back my health. Do you know how? Guess!' The young man guessed what I meant and lowered his eyes. 'So you have guessed. Depart in peace and sleep well.' I concluded. You see, I had to hold my tongue and let people guess what I meant, for the instant I presumed to play the friar people turned their backs upon me. I thought this information might serve to assist your readership with the journey of life and the calm of night-time.

Your obedient servant, James Makie, London, *1899*

A WHITE JACKAL

To the editor of The Times,

Sir, - Have any of your readers ever herd of a white, or rather cream coloured, jackel? I have killed one near the forests in this vicinity. It differs from the ordinary jackel on colour only, it being cream colour with brown markings. The natives inform me that they have seen jackles of this kind before, but state that they are very rare. Is it a new species or a freak of nature?

Yours truly, Eldame Ravine, Uganda. *12th Oct, 1902*

MOSQUITOES AND COLOUR

To the editor of The Herald,

Sir, - The very interesting notice of 'Mosquitoes and Colour' in your paper of this morning reminds me of an observation which I made many years ago when walking in Switzerland. I was much pestered by horse or cattle flies, to whom I am not an entomologist enough to assign their scientific name. These insects not only attacked my exposed face and hands, but assailed my legs, piercing through my knickerbocker stockings and causing me very serious annoyance. I chanced to notice, however, that when I used a brown umbrella as protection from the sun they settled on its large surface, while they did nothing of the kind on the white parasol of my companion; and this led me to substitute grey stockings for my reddish-brown ones with complete or almost complete success. I explained the matter to myself by supposing that the flies were attracted by the reddish-brown colour owing to its resemblance to that of their prey. The experiments, however, which you have described, show that this hastily adopted explanation was erroneous. For it appears that the most attractive colour of all to mosquitoes, and presumably to cattle-flies, is navy blue.

I am, Sir, your obedient servant, William Ogle, *2nd Sept, 1901*

TERRIBLE

To the editor of The Times,

Sir, - In addition to the improvements for omnibuses suggested in you recent column, I think the omnibus companies would find it to their advantage to provide a better system of lighting. At present many people are driven to using the underground means of conveyance owing to the impossibility of reading in an omnibus, what with the inefficient oil lamps in use. As I can't tolerate the underground means of transport, and consider the everyman on the omnibus to be retrograde, it would be a severe blow to me not to have the solace of reading.

I am, Sir, your obedient servant, J.H.H, *6th Nov, 1902*

THE ORDNANCE SURVEY

To the editor of The Gentleman,

Sir, - I would like to venture a suggestion on the subject of the sale of ordnance maps. I would propose that every post-office, which is also a telegraph office, should have in stock on sale for cash, copies of the map with a notification that it is for sale, and of the prices. There are several varieties of maps. They are, excluding editions now out of date: - 1. The contoured and hill-shaded map, with hills in brown. This is the best production of the survey, and the one most likely to attract the public. This should be displayed in the post-offices. It is my personal favorite. 2. The same map, with hills in black. 3. The contoured map, without hill-shading, known as the outline edition. 4. For certain districts the so-called map in colours, with red contours and blue water. This is an inferior impression of No.1. For the northern counties No.1 does not exist.

I am, Sir, yours very truly, Spencer Wilkinson
99 Oakley Street, S.W, *5th Sept, 1899*

THE SQUIRREL

To the editor of The Times,

Sir, - You permitted me two years ago to attack in The Times certain mistaken notions concerning squirrels, and perhaps you will permit me to record an observation which I have just made in reference to the same subject. A number of pine trees near here in recent high winds have shed so many twigs that the ground underneath is strewn by them, and a neighbour remarked to me, 'You see the work of your squirrels.' On examining the fallen twigs every one was found to be bored out by the pine beetle, and in one twig I found two specimens in full vigour. In my immediate neighbourhood the squirrels are not permitted to be molested, and the ground is covered under the pine trees in the most protected parts with the flakes of the pine cones thrown down by them as they eat the seeds. Under those trees so indicated as their haunts I have not found a single twig, and I have noticed that my own squirrels eat greedily the insects they find on the firs. The ground on which are the infested trees is separated by a broad, much travelled road from that in which live the squirrels, who never pass the road except to get water from a little lake which lies in the other side.

In my own little wood the squirrels are invited and fed, and firs, larches, chestnuts, and other trees are untouched by them. I hope this is of help.

Yours truly, W. J. Stillman.

Deepdene, Frimley Green, Surrey, *2nd Sept, 1899*

FEATURE
... Sex found me at four
Molly Parkin

Molly Parkin - fashion editor for the original Nova, originator of the trash sex novel, agony aunt and national icon - delves deep into her childhood, why she read Lolita and why, ultimately, oral sex with no teeth is the way forward.

There's nothing as self-satisfied as the smile on the chops of a so-retired sex symbol. I'm in my 70th year now, in the Departure Lounge of Immortality Airport, reliving past hedonism without those ancient terrors of unwanted pregnancy, of inconvenient disease, of tacky emotional entanglements. And how vividly enjoyable it all turns out to be on electrifying re-run.

Mae West claimed that the diary a girl keeps in her youth will one day keep her in old age. She was talking of hard cash. But she failed to mention the fact that erotic fantasies, when lived to the full in earlier years, can provide fodder for delicious dreams later on. Quite regularly these days I sail blithely through dawn on sumptuous orgasms all on my own, no hands, no help, nothing. Dead lovers paying nocturnal visitations? Sensual pleasures in spirit form. Sure.

These succulent memories keep me agog all day long. They are certainly sharper, more focused in my mind than where I've just placed my spectacles or, now toothless, my brand-new upper dentures. Only yesterday these pretty pearlies actually found their own way into the rubbish bin along with pear-peelings and a discarded perfume dispenser. I searched high and low, until family came hammering on the door. I opened up with a gummy grin and a throaty laugh, the true hag out of hell thing, and scared my grandchildren half-to-death. The psychic ten-year-old was the one who found the dentures in the end. I lure her into my den as often as I can just to oil the wheels of forgetfulness. I tell her I did the same for my own granny.

This isn't a new scenario for me; the frantic search for false teeth. I was called upon frequently, following sex, to track down the same for the oldest of my ancient lovers back in the '50s, an aristocratic octagenarian, who gave the tenderest of gob jobs. He certainly spoilt cunnilingus for me with younger stallions. Their strong white teeth - so harsh, so biting, so intrusive. Give me gums and a slack tongue any time.

It has been pertly suggested by, still-kittenish, pals of mine that I'd probably give sensational cock-suck on the same principle. But the appetite has gone. I prefer slathering on Toblerone, giant size I admit, not those mini-bars for toddlers which are now in the shops.

My own ageing has never held any dread for me. I always have had a penchant for the elderly and used to study everything I could about Gerontophilia when I decided that's what I had. An abnormal love for older bodies. My happiest childhood scenes are of sleeping in a feather bed at seven, between my grandparents, on the slope of our Welsh mountain back home. Awakening before the break of light, I'd sleepily watch my grandfather widdling into the wo-wo (family name for china potty) from under the bed, then swilling his face and hands in his own urine. I never questioned this or thought it strange in any way, obviously it was the only warm water in the house at that hour.

I mentioned it decades later to a herbal beautician when I was fashion editor at The Sunday Times. He had exquisite skin; an elderly Scottish scientist who had travelled down from the Highlands. I complimented him, saying that my grandfather's skin was as smooth and wrinkle-free too and I told him the wo-wo tale. He twinkled that fresh urine, blessed with magical minerals, was the best product anyone could use to maintain this kind of complexion. Yet, when I try to be helpful to the youth-and-image-obsessed by telling them this, they wrinkle up their noses and say it sounds like my usual disgusting gibberish. Some folk won't learn.

When my grandfather had left the bedroom to stoke a fire and prepare the porridge, steep the tea and butter the toast, before plucking one of his prize roses and bringing it all up to us on a tray, I took the precious time to study my sleeping grandmother. She obviously never, ever, swilled her skin in her urine or anyone else's. For her face, the most fascinating I had ever been this close to, wore an exquisite tracery of fine wrinkles and deep furrows. It looked like the handworked lace heirlooms handed down in our family. Womenfolk of my own blood who, through the centuries, had nothing better to do for hours on end than ruin their eyesight and spread their buttocks, cobwebbing these minute threaded miracles.

Yet as a corpse in her coffin, my granny was as smooth and unsullied as white marble. It was as if the undertaker had applied a steam-iron to her face. I truly thought that they must be burying the wrong cadaver until, that is, I recognised her sprigged Co-op nightie. The one I'd been sent down the road to buy with the Christmas dividend book. I'd been told to buy lavender, her favourite shade, but had been caught by the sprigs of bluebell instead.

I wasn't scolded when I got home. All my aunties crowded in from their various homes further down the road and said that the blue of the bluebells matched my granny's beautiful eyes and that the nightie was a wise choice and that I was blessed with good taste and an obvious love of flowers, inherited from my grandfather. He just smiled at me, so did my granny.

It was wartime, there was a blitz in London and I was living with them on loan until the war was over and my mother got herself together again. Their love for me was a wondrous thing, the warmth of it, their understanding that I suffered from an inability to follow instructions. I would want to do as I'd been asked but another way always beckoned. It was as if I was being guided to go against the herd, to build up a self protection and strength to guard against my own fallibility.

Sex found me at four. It came in the shape of my father, of his nudging erection as I sat in his lap on the stairs listening to my mother pounding out Beethoven on the piano in the locked parlour. We were far away from home, amongst our enemies, the English. We lived in one of the seedier London suburbs. We were Celts in a foreign country, my mother screamed more than once. Her misery made her hard to look at without wanting to run away. The words ripped her face in half until she was all teeth, snarling like the sheep dogs up in the mountain farm rounding the flocks. I understood already what the piano pounding really meant, more time spent with my father because my mother couldn't cope with anything, even me. Later she would spend increasing time in psychiatric wards, admitted after yet another attempt at suicide. I didn't mind this too much at the very start, it left me alone with a man who was showing me how to draw a turnip before turning it into a face. But after the first erection, there were inappropriate fondlings in the swimming pool, and straying fingers whilst teaching me to ride a bike. Then inexplicable rages enacted in my bedroom, harsh beatings followed by sentimental murmurings and embarrassing strokings. I was his "solace", he was always whispering that, whatever it meant. It was our secret and his instructions were never to tell. But in my 50s, decades after his demise, my mother long gone I showed my true colours, the inability to follow instructions. I spilled the beans. I let it all out.

"Hands up all those ladies who can recall their first erection, don't be shy now!" We all laughed, shy indeed, what tosh! Shyness didn't come into it, not on this self-empowerment seminar. Hands shot up, all 15 of us, pals now after the long weekend. Tales abounded of schoolyard pranks, furtive fumblings in the back of cars, cinema sex, sand up snatches, sticky fingers, uncircumcised dicks. At the very last came my turn.

"My fathers erection was my first." There was a subtle shift in the room. Utter silence. "I was four when sex found me," I finished quite lamely.

Uproar! Outrage! Group invective.

"You're a paedophile's daughter!" I was astonished, I had never thought of myself as that.

I've since read a lot about incest and about paedophilia, where before I felt physically sick at the mere sight of the words on the page. I started to read Lolita when it was first published and howled like a banshee in the locked bathroom. I couldn't finish it. I reread it last year and forced myself through to the end. But I squirmed, feeling myself the girlish object of lust again. A knowing child forced to feign innocence to retain her place in the pecking order of the peer group, prizing popularity to paper the cracks. Most sex symbols have suffered abuse in childhood, Monroe amongst them. She, the most potent sex symbol of them all.

Once, gathered around a high tea of beans on toast, and tinned peach slices with evaporated milk, my gaggle of aunties began gossiping about the twice-divorced femme fatale who had lured our most handsome uncle into holy matrimony. "No man was safe in the room with her," they tutted harsh judgement. "A passing glance from those sly eyes of hers and a man was a goner. All men are putty in her hands, poor dabs!"

I was 12 then and intrigued by this. My father had learnt to lay off me by then, physically and sexually that is, but he lashed me with his tongue, which felt more demoralising but less "dirty" at least. But the palpable lust was still there which meant that I could never remain alone with him in the same room. I had to be on my toes and ready to make a run for it at all times, until five years later, when my mother was away on family matters, my father and I were alone in the house and an event so sordid took place that there was no going forward or turning back. It had come to an end. I left home soon after. It was all over. I filed it away in the furthermost depths of me, marked "to remain unopened".

I gave what was left of my virginity to an older man, a famous actor, a household name. I look back on him now as the love of my life. His love had the quality of my grandparents' love. I choose to think that it is his passion that ignites my nights more than the others, the cast of hundreds which most sex symbols can boast.

I have forgiven my father now. I love him again. I am compassionate in asking myself how much more wretched he must have felt than even me. I've wiped the slate clean. I can even thank him for the femme fatale years when I wrecked revenge on all men, when no member of the opposite sex was safe with me around. Like the siren so deplored, so envied by my aunties. They never aimed any such criticism at me, quite the opposite.

"There she goes, our lovely girl, our very own sex symbol ■"

REFLECTION

... Inside Out
Victoria Miro

Victoria Miro, the international art dealer based in London looks towards herself rather than the canvas.

When I finished my studying at the Slade and Reading university, I taught, but found I was drifting away from art itself.

Now I am a dealer, having had a gallery in Cork Street for fifteen years and now a large gallery space off City Road, London. I started the gallery because I wanted to have a life in art, not business, and teaching was not enough. I wanted to nurture artists and present them to the outside world. Hopefully the new gallery will be seen as some kind of small private institution; a place to look at art quietly, away from worldly problems. I love making exhibitions. I like engaging with people through my business, especially as I can wear many hats, mixing rich with poor, and be able to converse in any country. The positive responses from people, the discussions and shared interests fuel me with energy. I would not want any other kind of life. Fashion is especially interesting when it does reflect the identity of a person. I wear clothes that please me aesthetically and like the art I show, I hope they express something of my inner self. I do strive to maintain a veneer of tranquillity and experience has taught me to put problems into context, but I am not as passive as I appear.

I love being alone and having time for inner dialogue. It is not so much that I am secretive, but enjoy my inner life and this can lead to people sensing a lack of communication on my part. Still discretion is a vital ingredient in my work. I never reveal the books I read and I never take family snapshots - I prefer to draw upon my own special memory bank. Sometimes I talk to strangers, especially when travelling and I like to elicit their ideas outside of my immediate world. When I am abroad I feel somehow liberated, often finding a greater reaction and understanding to the art I love ∎

MONOLOGUE

... What do people say given half the chance?
Reverend Paul Bowtell

My first memory was being pushed in a buggie on Rose Green, Bognor Regis, England. I will have been one or two. I can't say it was an easy time then, what with emotional problems and general family hardship. For this reason I can't recall very much. I have difficulty with some people's belief that they can remember being born. Having said that I do fully accept that those memories are somewhere inside of us, and that in certain situations we can take ourselves back to that point, through therapy for example. I mean, it's one of the most dramatic points of our lives, being brought into the trauma of the world from the comfort and protection of the womb. And there's the potential for further trauma, of complications with the birth, or simply the child not receiving comfort from the mother, say if she is ill. From this there can be a real sense of rejection. I think the experiences from this early stage really are part of life, whether we remember it or not. Life begins from conception.

I came to the church I currently read at through a calling to work with the Christian worshipping community. Also to help people who are facing difficulties, to strengthen them and encourage them to look for God. I am here firstly for the sake of the individuals, who are following Christ, but secondly for the corporate expression of the church, reaching out and offering the love of Christ to the community around. We have an 18 bed rehab downstairs in the crypt, where I give spiritual guidance to the, well, they are typically men with drinking problems, or we offer help to the prostitutes - legal and, again, spiritual. We offer help in a holistic way: which means to tackle people's problems in an entire, complete way.

Genetics is difficult for a Christian to deal with, as we are the product of, and are cared for by, God. Lots of children are born into a broken world. Well, our world is broken, things do go wrong. We all have to struggle with the thought that if there is a God then why are some children born with defects. Of course there are many instances where the parents would never want to change the process of their children being born with a defect, due to the joy the child has with the world, which is a very real joy for the parents. That it was not something to be rubbished. Should there be an arian race? Do I agree with genetic engineering? I have to say that we are tinkering with the preserve of God here. Although I must say that I have never had to deal with any major genetic imperfections in life (for example with my children), and I think that does make a difference. Recently developed and almost realised computers which think, which have consciousness, I am not too worried about. I do like Hal in 2001. But there's a uniqueness in mankind which is the ability to have a relationship with God. This will never be the case with computers. Medicine and drugs should not be in the hands of the multinationals, but should be made more available to the sick. If there were greater availability there would be less of an Aids crisis, for example. As a species, I think we are not changing. We're becoming cleverer at protecting ourselves, at killing and getting more self-sufficient. Still, we also see marvelous glimmers of hope where people choose the community over the individual. I might be wrong but I do sense that in the past this happened more, that there was a greater sense of community and less emphasis on the self.

I don't expect mankind will end up with a utopia. If I go with what I read from the Bible then we have the last chapter, the Revelation, which talks about Armageddon; the present world being wrapped up, finished, and a beginning of a new heaven and a new earth. My hope lies in the fact that this is not the only life. C.S. Lewis said that this world is like the ante room leading into the great banquet hall, and we are but waiting here for the greater reality which is to come. We can begin to touch that greater reality in a spiritual way. This is where my hope lies, even though I don't mind getting my hands dirty here, in this world.

I like the Moody Blues, they were one of the first bands to make concept albums. I also like the Rolling Stones very much. Celebrity seems to be about heroes, role models, people we can look up to. Fashion is about the importance of developing the exterior. We place importance on this as deep down within us we experience a disturbance, a brokenness. So as we can't easily change that, we attempt to change the outside, the surface. Which is a way of recognising that we have sin in our lives, that there is a need to change, to acquire forgiveness for the guilt we have. Fashion is a way to cope, it's what we do: God gave us fashion to enjoy, good clothes and colours are pleasing. One can only glimpse beauty briefly, and if you try to own it, it disappears. Perhaps that's why it's free. It's also innocent, which is perhaps another reason why it's so fleeting, as we are not ▪

Reverend Paul is reader of Christs Church, Spitalfields, East London.

INTERVIEW

By Georges Belmont

Marilyn Monroe

> *This interview, published by Marie Claire in 1960, was Monroe's last. It shows her as a thoughtful, warm and focused woman, not the dumb, blonde cliché people like to believe. This is the Marilyn who so captivated Truman Capote and W.J. Weatherby that they each published records of their conversations with her some years after her death.*

MARILYN MONROE: I'd much rather answer questions. I simply can't tell the whole story, that's terrible... Where to begin? How? There are so many twists and turns.
GEORGES BELMONT: *Still, it began somewhere. What are your earliest childhood memories?*
MARILYN MONROE: It's the memory of a struggle for survival. I was still very small - a baby in a little bed, yes, and I was struggling for life. But I'd rather not talk about it if it's all the same to you. It's a cruel story, and it's no one's business but my own as I said.

It's true that I was illegitimate. My mother's first husband was named Baker. Her second was Mortenson.
Anyway my name was Norma Jean Baker. It was in all my school records. Everything else that's been said is crazy.

During the war I worked in a factory. The work was boring and it was pretty awful there. The other girls would talk about what they'd done the night before and what they were going to do the next weekend. I worked where the paint sprayers were nothing but men. They used to stop their work to write me notes.

And then one day the Air Force wanted to take pictures of our factory. I worked as a model here and there for several days, holding things in my hand, pushing things around, pulling them...

The pictures were developed at Eastman Kodak and the people there asked who the model was and one of the photographers - David Conover - came back and said to me, 'You should be a model. You'd easily earn $5 an hour.' $5 an hour! I was earning $20 a week for 10 hours a day and I had to stand all day on a concrete floor. Reason enough to give it a try. And I was able to pursue one of my dreams. From time to time I took drama lessons, when I had enough money. They were expensive; I paid $10 an hour.

There are a lot of stories told about those calendar pictures. When the story came out, I'd already done Asphalt Jungle and was rehired at Fox with a seven-year contract. I still remember the publicity department calling me on the set and asking, 'Did you pose for a calendar?' And I said, 'Yes, anything wrong?' Well they were real anxious and they said, 'Don't say you did, say you didn't.' I said, 'But I did, and I signed the release, so I feel I should say so.' They were very unhappy about that. And then the cameraman on the film got hold of one of the calendars and asked me if I'd sign it, and so I said yes, I would. And I said, 'This isn't my best angle you know.' And the studio got even madder.

Anyone who knows me knows that I can't lie. Sometimes I leave things out or I don't want to elaborate, to protect myself or other people - who probably don't even want to be protected - but I can never tell a lie.

People are funny. They ask me a question and when you're honest, they're shocked. Someone once asked me, 'What do you wear in bed? Pyjama tops? Bottoms? Or a nightgown?' So I said 'Chanel No. 5.' Because it's the truth. You know, I don't want to say 'nude', but it's the truth.

There came the time when I began to, let's say, 'be known', and nobody could imagine what I did when I wasn't shooting because they didn't see me at previews or premieres or parties. It's simple. I was going to school. I'd never finished high school, so I started going to UCLA at night, because during the day I had small parts in pictures. I took courses in the history of literature and the history of this country, and I started to read a lot, stories by wonderful writers.

It was hard to get to classes on time because I worked in the studio till 6.30pm and since I had to get up early to be ready for shooting at 9.00am. I was tired and sometimes I would fall asleep in the classroom. But I forced myself to sit up and listen.

The professor, Mrs Seay, didn't know who I was and found it odd that the boys from other classes often looked through the window during our class and whispered to one another. One day she asked about me and they said, 'She's a movie actress.' And she said, 'Well I'm very surprised. I thought she was a young girl just out of a convent.' That was one of the nicest compliments I ever got.

But the people I just talked about, they liked to see me as a starlet; so frivolous and dumb.

I have a reputation for being late. Well, I don't think I'm late all the time. People just remember the times I come too late. Besides, I really don't think I can go as fast as other people. They get in their cars, they run into each other, they never stop. I don't think mankind was intended to be like machines.

My problem is that I drive myself, but I do want to be wonderful, you know? I know some people may laugh about that, but it's true.

There's a book by Rainer Maria Rilke that's helped me a lot, Letters To A Young Poet. Without it I'd probably think I was crazy sometimes. I think that when an artist - forgive me, but I do think I'm becoming an artist, even though some people will laugh; that's why I apologise - when an artist tries to be true you sometimes feel you're on the verge of some kind of craziness. But it isn't really craziness. You're just trying to get the truest part of yourself out, and it's very hard, you know.

I always have this secret feeling that I'm really a fake or something, a phoney. Everyone feels that way now and then, I guess. My teacher, Lee Strasberg at the Actors' Studio, often asks me, 'Why do you feel that way about yourself? You're a human being.' I answer, 'Yes, I am, but I feel like I have to be more.' 'No,' he says, 'you have to start with yourself. What are you doing?' I said, 'Well, I have to get into a part.' He says, 'No, you're a human being so you start with yourself.' 'With me?' I shouted the first time he said that. 'Yes, with you!'

I think Lee probably changed my life more than any other human being. That's why I love to go to the Actor's Studio whenever I'm in New York. My one desire is to do my best, the best that I can from the moment the camera starts until it stops. That moment I want to be perfect, as perfect as I can make it.

Love and work are the only things that really happen to us. Everything else doesn't really matter. I think that one without the other isn't so good - you need both. When I married Joe DiMaggio in 1954, he had already retired from baseball, but he was a wonderful athlete and had a very sensitive nature in many respects. His family were immigrants and he'd had a difficult time when he was young. So he understood something about me, and I understood something about him, and we based our marriage on this. But just 'something' isn't enough. Our marriage wasn't very happy and it ended in nine months.

My feelings are as important to me as my work. Probably that's why I'm so impetuous and exclusive. I like people but when it comes to friends, I only like a few. And when I love, I'm so exclusive that I really have only one idea in my mind.

Above all, I want to be treated as human being.

When I met Arthur Miller the first time it was on a set, and I was crying. I was playing in a picture called As Young As You Feel, and he and Elia Kazan came over to me. I was crying because a friend of mine had died. I was introduced to Arthur. I was in love with him from that moment.
Since we've been married we lead a happy life in New York. Now and then the actors from the studio will come over and I'll give them breakfast or tea, and we'll study while we eat. So my days are pretty full. But the evenings are always free for my husband.

After dinner we often go to the theatre or to a movie, or we have friends in, or we visit friends. Often we just stay home, listen to music, talk, read. Or we go for a walk after dinner in Central Park, sometimes; we love to walk. We don't have a set way of doing things. There are times when I would like to be more organised than I am, to do certain things at certain times. But my husband says at least it never gets dull. So it's all right. I'm not bored by things; I'm just bored by people who are bored.

I like people, but sometimes I wonder how sociable I am. I can easily be alone and it doesn't bother me. I don't mind it, it's like a rest, it kind of refreshes my self. I think there are two things about human beings - at least, I think there are about me: they want to be alone and they also want to be together. I have a gay side to me and also a sad side. That's a real problem. I'm very sensitive to that. That's why I love my work. When I'm happy with it, I feel more sociable. If not, I like to be alone. And in my private life, it's the same way.

If I asked you what does it feel like being Marilyn Monroe, at this stage in your life, what would you answer?

Well how does it feel being yourself?

Sometimes I'm content with myself, at other times I'm dissatisfied.

That's exactly how I feel. And are you happy?

I think so.

Well I am too, and since I'm only 34 and have a few years to go yet, I hope to have time to become better and happier, professionally and in my personal life. That's my one ambition. Maybe I'll need a long time, because I'm slow. I don't want to say that it is the best method, but it's the only one I know and it gives me the feeling that, in spite of everything, life is not without hope ▪

FICTION
... Bodywork
Hari Kunzru

Hi Ho
Sunday mornings I wash my car. The house is on the brow of a hill, so while I run the chamois over the Sierra's shiny curves I can look over the allotments and see other early birds clearing and digging their little patches of dirt. I've never been much of a one for gardening. All that muck. If there's been one thing constant in my life it's that I've always liked to keep things neat. Of course, round here it doesn't do to let it slip too far, so after I've done the car I usually spray the front lawn, walking a little circuit with a canister of weedkiller on my back. Hi ho!

Sunday mornings are my own. Cheryl never raises her head before 10.30am, refuses to. Sometimes she'll say she's 'a little indisposed'. Times I've brought her a cup of tea, trying to chivvy her up for some day trip we've planned, and found her wrapped up in the bed clothes looking up at the ceiling. Quite awake mind you. Just far away.

No daytrip today. I went out to the ringroad, to the Superstore.

A List
1. 15 metres rubber tubing (ultrafine) **2.** 'Darco' (?) Bearings (x4) **3.** 5x5m Plastic laminate **4.** Screws, bolts, washers, nuts etc. (various) **5.** Aleph Industries 'Victor' pump (size 4) **6.** Gold wire (2oz wound) **7.** 1 ltr SuperGrade lubricant **8.** Fittings SA9858674a (x4), SA985867b (3), SD945536a (1), SX966632a, b, c (3 of each) **9.** Roehmer-Sharpe dissection scalpel set (cat. A4765) **10.** Sutures (RS cat. S3367) **11.** Local anaesthetic 'Devorine' (25x5ml ampoules - Untergang SA or unbranded equivalent) **12.** Sterile pads (RS cat. C35) **13.** Tourniquet (or make one?) **14.** SynaptoKit™ **15.** Skin 2000™ **16.** Other (ask).

Pretty Girl
Indeed she was, in her blue and white striped uniform. She helped me put the things in the boot. I smiled at her, hoping she would smile back. And she did. Looked like a photograph I once saw in a magazine.

Favour
Afterwards I drove round to TD Repairs. I've got a mate fixes things. Vacuum cleaners, tellies, radios, you name it. Barry, he said, take whatever you need. He showed me round the back, where he keeps the bits he's taken out. Left me to have a good old rummage around. I offered to pay him, but he wouldn't hear of it. Lovely bloke, Ted. I'd picked out quite a lot, circuit boards and so on. Still, he wouldn't take a penny.

Back Home
There are instructions to follow. It looks a little daunting, until you take the plunge. I lay all the stuff out on the table in the garage - I haven't got a proper workshop, one of the drawbacks of the house. And it's important to keep things clean, especially with something like this, which is hard to do in the garage. Reluctantly I decide to keep the Sierra outside until I've got it finished. All that oil, not to mention the stuff it picks up on the wheels. When I go back inside for the bucket and mop I realise Cheryl's still not up. It's past 12.00pm which, even for her, is unheard of.

All the curtains are drawn

  'Are you ill love? What's the matter?'

  She doesn't answer. I notice there's a funny smell in the room, sort of sweet. So I open the window, let a bit of air in.

  'Well, what is it, love? It's almost lunchtime.'

  'Go away,' she says. 'I'm fine.'

Step by Step
Choose a small square of tissue on the left forearm, just below the elbow. Make an incision on three sides (fig 1.13) taking care to cut no deeper than the layer of subcutaneous fat. Peel back and sprinkle with powder from the sachet provided. Taking your precut square of laminate, affix it to the opened section, holding in place until it has fully adhered to the epidermis. Cover and leave. Repeat this over the whole forearm area until (fig 1.14) you have exposed the area shaded grey. You are now ready to isolate the flexor muscles, in preparation for the first series of implants.

Connections
receptor Eu.306.56 V CNS site 56 (red)
receptor Eu.306.57 V CNS site 56 (cyan)
receptor Eu.306.58 V CNS site 56 (magenta)
receptor Eu.306.59 V CNS site 56 (blue)
receptor Eu.306.00 V CNS site 57 (red)
receptor Eu.307.01 V CNS site 57 (cyan)
receptor Eu.307.02 V CNS site 58 (red)
receptor Eu.307.03 V CNS site 59 (red)
receptor Eu.307.04 V CNS site 59 (cyan)
receptor Eu.307.05 V CNS site 60 (blue only)

Mixed Feelings
Cheryl and I have our ups and downs. At the moment I suppose we're going through a low patch. Not to worry. In spite of what's happening I have reason to feel quite pleased. I'm proud of myself, actually, and I hope she will be too. It's a fiddly job, but I'm proving myself more than a match for it. Both the arms are finished. I can touch my face and feel the spongy finger pads, my designer fingers, touching my cheek. They smell of hi-fi showrooms, or the plastic covers on the upholstery of new cars.

Domestic Trouble?

No. Certainly not. We have what you might call a happy marriage. Contented. I've always taken care to see that Cheryl has a few nice things, and she in her turn has provided for me as a wife should. There are those who say that in the modern world our sort of marriage is out of date. But my Cheryl's never had need of anything. She knows I care for her. And that's enough. It's our anniversary, as it happens. 23 years today. We're going to a restaurant.

Le Pont d'Avignon

The waiter is decent enough. Often they'll hover round you, fluster you as you try to choose. Cheryl speaks some French, though as usual at the moment she isn't saying anything. When the wine comes she makes a grab for her glass, knocks it back and tells him to fill her up again. I am extremely embarrassed. This is not the Cheryl I know. He says something funny to her with madame on the end of it and she giggles like a bloody schoolgirl. Tosses back another glassful, and then belches. I decide I should say something.

'Pull yourself together Cheryl. You're making a spectacle of yourself.'

'Shut up,' she says. She actually tells me to shut up, right there in the restaurant. And the waiter can hear too. Bastard starts sniggering to the girl who takes your coat.

'Cheryl!' Between my teeth, like. 'Why are you doing this?'

As I say it I notice how she smells. Normally, she wears a little perfume, smells fresh and clean as spring. But tonight Cheryl smells sweet, rotten sweet like something you've left out of the fridge too long. It's quite disgusting. And she's sweating. Her face is shiny and damp.

'Look Cheryl. Love. It's obvious you're not well. We'd better be getting home.'

And she starts to laugh again.

'Not well, is it? Take a look at me, Barry. What is it you see?'

'Don't Cheryl. You're playing games. You know I don't like it.'

'Come on love,' Just like that. Sneering. 'Come on love, answer me.'

'I don't know. You, Cheryl. I see you.'

'I don't think you see anything at all, love. But there's someone here, Barry, a human being.' And she begins to laugh. 'A human being that's just pissed itself.'

I will never forget how she looks at this moment, her sweaty face split open by that horrible grin. Cheryl, *My Wife*, looks disgusting, dirty. I get up to leave, trying to pull my wallet out of my jacket. I just want to go. She never uses that sort of language, never. I tell myself she's ill, doesn't know what she's doing. But at the same time I realise there's a side to her I didn't know before, a crude side. And I'm afraid. I don't even notice if she's following me as I stuff a £20 note into the waiter's hand. As she comes towards the car, I notice she was telling the truth. Her skirt is soaking wet, a great dark patch across the front. I twist the key in the ignition and drive away, leaving her standing there in the car park. Laughing at me.

1.47AM

Lingual sites are divided into four areas, roughly corresponding to the traditional distinctions between sweet, sour, bitter and salt (Fig. 32.4) To configure the unit, simply connect the input device to the temporary ports marked 'a' through 'e'. Key in the following strings to install default settings...

A Letter

Dear Cheryl. What is happening to us? I know that lately things have not been too good but tonight has made me worried about the future. I wish you would tell me what is happening and if I have done anything to you. It seems we are so far apart, we are both mature adult people, Cheryl, and we should talk it over. Lets get this thing straightened out.

Out. Out in the open. Let's put it on the table. Put our feelings...

It took me hours to work up to that. Hours just sitting in the garage with my head in my hard new hands. And now it doesn't seem quite right. I screw the paper up and throw it into the bin in the corner of the garage. I have to be careful not to make any big movements because I'm still hooked up to the little box.

a100Xon, a1200Xoff, a14400Xon, a144800Xoff, b100Xoff, b120Xoff, b2000Xon, b2200Xon, b11000(0), b12000(0), b12250(0), b14400Xon...

I'm staying put, right here in the garage. Been here all night, wasn't able to go to bed. I don't know what to do, because I can't stomach being in the same room with her. The stench is unbearable.

She's my wife.

I was in the garden, some time after midnight, looking in through the kitchen window. There she was, in her nightie, drinking a glass of water. Everything, everything underneath seemed to be rippling, moving about as if it were alive. I was horrified. What's become of her? What's going to become of us?

When I crept up to bed she must have been asleep. Waves of it, that rotten toilet smell, coming off her. The night light was still on, and she had one arm over the covers, the sleeve of her nightie all rucked up. The arm was all moist with sweat, seemed to be pouring out of her in buckets. I tried to get closer to the bed and found my heart was racing, like I was going to have a seizure. I felt it was going to hammer its way out of my chest.

Pink.

The droplets of sweat. On her arm. They were pink, like they were mixed with blood.

Fiddly Bits

There are parts which are difficult to do yourself. I obviously couldn't ask Cheryl, so I gave Ted a ring. In a way I think he was quite flattered, and he came over as soon as you like. Having made the various preparations, some of which made me rather woozy, we pried open the chest cavity and got to work. I was glad of his help. He's nimble-fingered, old Ted, fitted the litle sacs and tubes and whatnot onto the pump and before I'd really had time to draw breath (ha ha), we were having a swift half round the corner.

'Bit sore I expect Barry.'

I must admit I didn't answer right off. I was far away. Preoccupied, to tell the truth. Something not quite right. I'd been looking forward to that pint, and now it tasted strange. Sort of metallic. I said as much to Ted.

'Why don't you send it back? Oi Derek! Derek!'

'Shut it, Ted!'

'I'm sorry?'

'Leave it alone, eh. Maybe there's nothing up with it. I'd rather you didn't.'

"Alright old son. No need to get all aggravated.'

I had to apologise to him after that. He took it well. Not one to hold a grudge, Ted. Promised to come back after work the next day and help me with the intestines.

Upstairs

I pulled back the covers. Cheryl is out, God knows where. I pulled back the covers and saw the brown stain her body had left from last night. There are stains on her clothes too, and in the bath there's a mat of hair. Her clothes stink of rotten meat. Holding my breath I shoved some of them into a bin bag. Then I walked down to the bottom of the garden and burnt them.

Signs of Decay

I know Cheryl has been back, because there's blood in the toilet. Since Ted and I had that stint last week I haven't actually needed to use it myself. I just went in to check on her. A sort of red mist in the water. Since I try to be in the garage whenever she's about I don't see her any more. I just find the signs. Everything's on the floor of the bedroom. The kitchen looks like a bomb has hit it, pans with food stuck to the bottom, spilt something or other on the linoleum, rotting vegetables on the side. It's coming into the hot weather. The flies are buzzing round it. Breeding ground. But as I say, since last week it's none of my concern.

Bit bothered to notice some scarring on the knees. In the manual it says the material's resistant, and I've hardly been doing anything too strenuous. God alone knows what would happen if I took it into my head to go rockclimbing, or play football. I was wondering about taking them back, getting a refund, but to be honest I can't be bothered. I suppose that's what they count on, that you can't be bothered. They're on, and they'll stay on.

Anticipation

When I get dirty I just take a cloth and wipe the surfaces down. Smooth, perfect. I can even shine them if I want to. A plastic skin, a barrier between me and all the muck and filth outside. Now there are only a few things left to do, but they're the hardest ones. You have to buy the module as a unit, comes from America. Though Cheryl doesn't know it, I've been saving up for some time. A little bit here, a little bit there. And now it's unpacked, little twists of polystyrene dotted about on the workbench. I'm excited. Look at the time, Ted'll be round any minute.

Section 275.12

Both UniSys™ interior and posterior choroid plexus sets come ready configured for use with any US Standard CNS kit. Slots are available for all major intramodular interfaces. If you find problems initialising the units please refer to the troubleshooting guide at the rear of this manual.

This is it.

The most important stage. After this everything will flow in straight lines. No mess and no confusion. I'll always know what to do because the answers will be there inside. Neat rows of electrons stacked like soldiers on parade. Yes-no, yes-no, yes-no. I'm excited, and why not? This is it. The last fuzzy bit of me is about to fall away. I'll be as clean and bright and perfect as a racing car. All the dead stuff falling off me like leaves in autumn.

Well, will you look at that. It's not often I get poetic. Never was one for it at school. The-boy-stood-on-the-burning-deck and so on. Doesn't usually do much for me. What could have brought it on now? The excitement, I expect. Will I still get excited, after? Will I still think of things like autumn leaves? Won't be any need, most probably .

This is it. This - is - it. After tonight I should know what to do with Cheryl too. I saw her today, first time in weeks. Awful. She'd smeared herself in her own - anyway, I couldn't bear to look at her. I can hear her now, upstairs in the bathroom. There's a damp patch spreading across the ceiling. Not to worry. Not to worry. The unit is sitting there on the table, unpacked and ready to be popped in. Ted will be round in a minute, and after that it will all be plain sailing ▪

The Impressionist is published by Hamish Hamilton / Penguin (UK) May 2002 and simultaneously by Dutton in the US.

Maria Runyantseva, Author

Harland Miller, Author

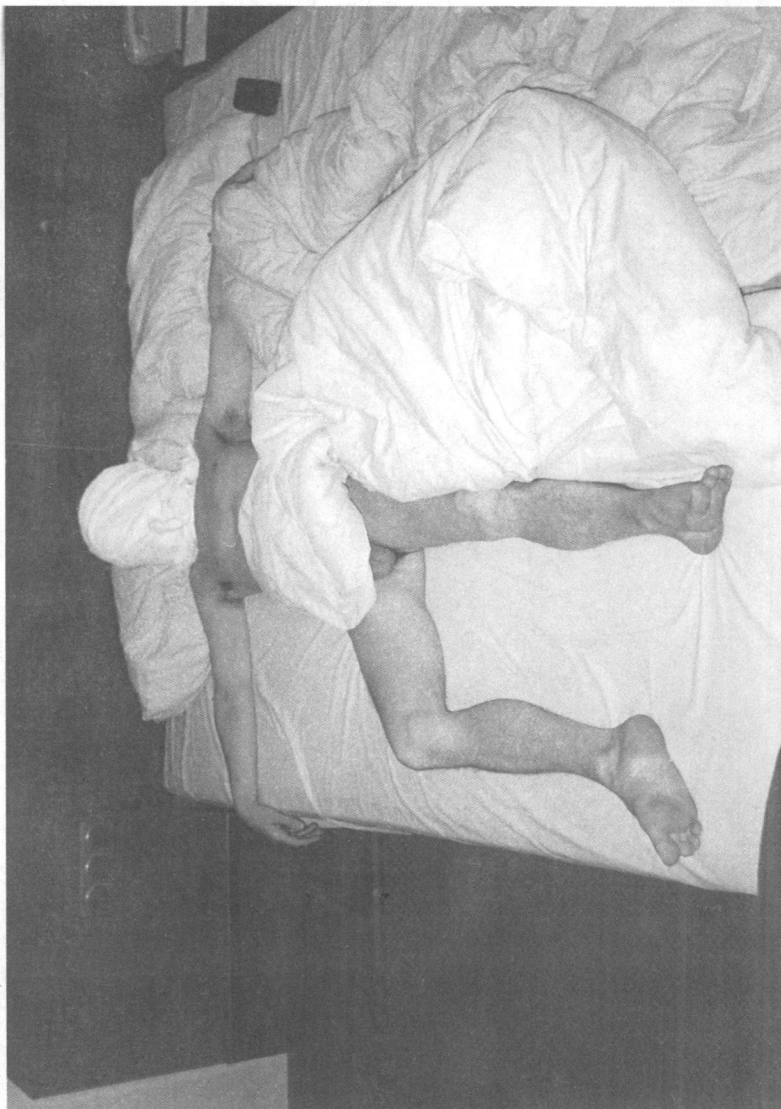

To: Mark Kostabi
       555 West 25th Street
       New York, NY 10001, USA

ADDING, SUBTRACTING (August 25, 2000)

It is good to remember that art is sinful for the same reason that homicide and suicide are: they all dabble in divine creation by adding to, or subtracting from God's art. It is also good to remember that the jealous bastard is even more jealous when it comes to adding than subtracting. An artist through and through, God.

From: Ranko Bon, 11 Abbot's Walk, Reading RG1 3HW, UK, Phone: +44 (0) 118 9504490, E-mail: R.Bon@reading.ac.uk, Web: www.residua.org

Returned For Better Address

BY AIR MAIL
par avion
                    Royal Mail

Ranko Bon, Postcard Terrorist

Jake Arnott, Author

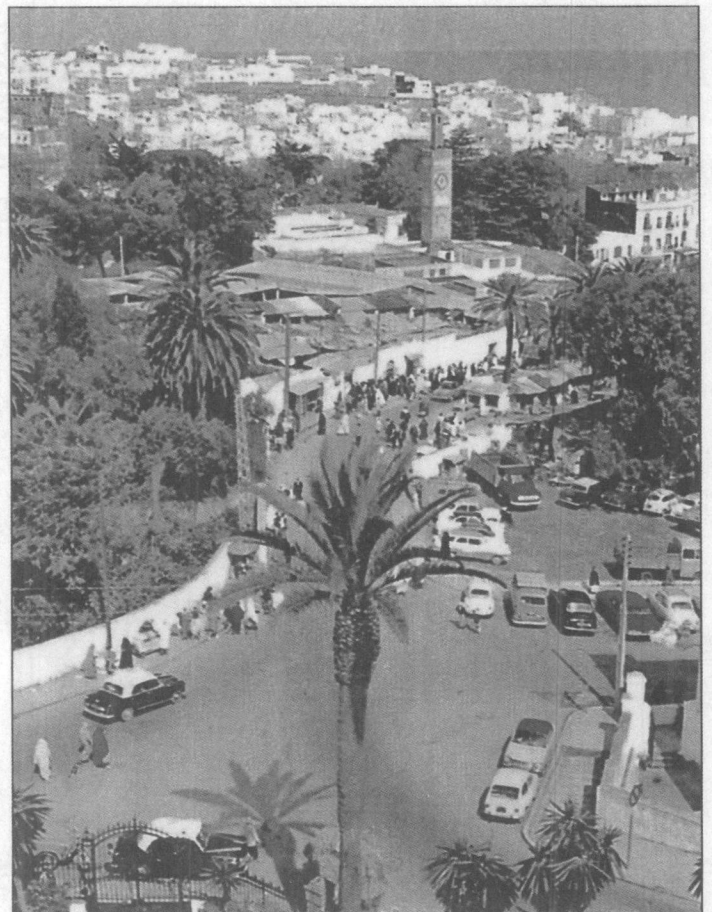

Tanger

POSTCARD

To: Dan Crowe
Another Magazine
112 Old Street
London EC1

NINE REASONS FOR BEING HAPPY (March 24, 2001)

In the Seventeenth Century, Ting Shiung Fei listed nine reasons for being happy following Lai Chu Tang's example several generations back. In his commentary, Taoist master Chang Shing Kung also listed nine reasons for being happy, but most of them were exactly the opposite of those cited by Ting and Lai. Leaving Ting, Lai, and Chang behind, I, too, will list nine reasons for being happy: (1) I am reading many books but writing only one; (2) I have several wives but they all live apart from me and each other; (3) I like to drink good wine but I am happy with only a bottle a day; (4) I enjoy playing chess although I play it rather poorly; (5) a surprisingly large number of people care about me and, perhaps even more surprisingly, I care about them, too; (6) I neither have nor need a teacher; (7) I travel lightly and find beauty everywhere I go; (8) I am rarely ill but I enjoy illness whenever I succumb to it; and (9) in my mid-fifties, I worry neither about my own livelihood nor that of my children.

To Annabel Campigotto

From: Ranko Bon, 11 Abbot's Walk, Reading RG1 3HW, UK, Phone: +44 (0) 118 9504490, E-mail: R.Bon@reading.ac.uk, Web: www.residua.org

---

Москва. Кремлевская звезда.
Moscow. Kremlin Star.

c/o DAN CROWE
ANOTHER MAGAZINE
112-116 OLD STREET
LONDON, ANGLIA
LONDON EC1V 9BG
UNITED KINGDOM

TANGER (Maroc)
Vue Partielle

In a trance dance of tangerine dreaming Tanger is a tired old hustler of a city. An international zone of the mind. A tart with a lot of heart. Inshallah.

RAIMAGE S.A.R.L.
2, Rue de la Russie - Tél.: 039 93 42 02 - TANGER

© Raimage
RAISSOUNI IMAGE

[REF: 013]

Dan Crowe
Another Magazine
112-116 Old Street
LONDON EC1V 9BG
ANGLETERRE

Like most people who at some time in their lives have said with joy or incredulity: I wish my friends could see me now (which perhaps shortens to the postcard favourite: wish you were here!) I've also wished that self-same thing. Equally though there've been times - less than a few but more than enough - when I've been glad they couldn't. This German reading tour has turned into just one of those times.

Love Howard

EXTRACT 1
... Orlando
Virginia Woolf

Orlando, published in 1928, was not Woolf's most famous work, but it was one of her most intense considerations of gender, and how it evolved in Europe over the course of 400 years.

And as she drove, we may seize the opportunity, since the landscape was of a simple English kind which needs no description, to draw the reader's attention more particularly than we could at the moment to one or two remarks which have slipped in here and there in the course of the narrative. For example, it may have been observed that Orlando hid her manuscripts when interrupted. Next, that she looked long and intently in the glass; and now, as she drove to London, one might notice her starting and suppressing a cry when the horses galloped faster than she liked. Her modesty as to her writing, her vanity as to her person, her fears for her safety all seem to hint that what was said a short time ago about there being no change in Orlando the man and Orlando the woman, was ceasing to be altogether true. She was becoming a little more modest, as woman are, of her brains, and a little more vain, as woman are, of her person. Certain susceptibilities were asserting themselves, and others were diminishing. The change of clothes had, some philosophers will say, much to do with it. Vain trifles as they seem, clothes have, they say, more important offices than merely to keep us warm. They change our view of the world and the world's view of us. For example, when Captain Bartolus saw Orlando's skirt, he had an awning stretched for her immediately, pressed her to take another slice of beef, and invited her to go ashore with him in the long boat. These compliments would not have been paid her had her skirts, instead of flowing, been cut tight to her legs in the fashion of breeches. And when we are paid compliments, it behoves us to make some return. Orlando curtseyed; she complied; she flattered the good man's humours as she would not have done had his neat breeches been a woman's skirts, and his braided coat a woman's satin bodice. Thus, there is much to support the view that it is clothes that wear us and not we them; we may make them take the mould of arm and breast, but they mould our hearts, our brains, our tongues to their liking. So, having now worn skirts for a considerable time, a certain change was visible in Orlando, which is to be found if the reader will look at plate 5, even in her face. If we compare the picture of Orlando as a man with that of Orlando as a woman we shall see that though both are undoubtedly one and the same person, there are certain changes. The man has his hands free to seize his sword, the woman must use hers to keep the satins from slipping from her shoulders. The man looks the world full in the face, as if it was made for his use and fashioned to his liking. The woman takes a sidelong glance at it, full of suspicion. Had they both worn the same clothes, it is possible that their outlook might have been the same.

That is the view of some philosophers and wise ones, but on the whole, we incline to another. The difference between the sexes is, happily, one of great profundity. Clothes are but a symbol of something hid deep beneath. It was a change in Orlando herself that dictated her choice of a woman's dress and of a woman's sex. And perhaps in this she was only expressing rather more openly than usual - openness indeed was the soul of her nature - something that happens to most people without thus being plainly expressed. For here again, we come to a dilemma. Different though the sexes are, they intermix. In every human being a vacillation from one sex to the other takes place, and often it is only the clothes that keep the male or female likeness, while underneath the sex is the very opposite of what is above. Of the complications and confusions which thus result everyone has had experience; but here we leave the general question and note only the odd effect it had in the particular case of Orlando herself.

For it was this mixture in her of a man and a woman, one being uppermost and the other, that often gave her conduct an unexpected turn. The curious of her own sex would argue, for example, if Orlando was a woman, how did she never take more than ten minutes to dress? And were not her clothes chosen rather at random, and sometimes worn rather shabby? And then they would say, still, she has none of the formality of a man, or a man's love of power. She is excessively tender hearted. She could not indure to see a donkey beaten or a kitten drowned. Yet again, they noted, she detested household matters, was up at dawn and out among the fields in the summer before the sun had risen. No farmer knew more about the crops than she did. She could drink with the best and liked games of hazard. She rode well and drove six horses at a gallop over London Bridge. Yet again, though bold and active as a man, it was remarked that the sight of another in danger brought on the most womanly palpitations. She would burst into tears on slight provocation. She was unversed in geography, found mathematics intolerable, and held some caprices which are more common among woman than men, as for instance that to travel south is to travel downhill. Whether, then, Orlando was most man or woman, it is difficult to say and cannot now be decided. For her coach was now rattling on the cobbles. She had reached her home in the city. The steps were being let down; the iron gates were being opened. She was entering her fathers house at Blackfriars, which though fashion was fast deserting that end of town, was still a pleasant, roomy mansion, with gardens running down to the river, and a pleasant grove of nut trees to walk in.

EXTRACT 2

... Lolita

Vladimir Nabokov

This extract, taken from Lolita and banned until Olympia Press published it in 1955 caused mass outrage on both sides of the Atlantic. It also established Nabokov as one of the greatest writers of the 20th century. In 1964, Girodas, the owner of Olympia Press, was banned from publishing in France.

She had entered my world, umber and black Humberland, with rash curiosity; she surveyed it with a shrug of amused distaste; and it seemed to me now that she was ready to turn away from it with something akin to plain repulsion. Never did she vibrate under my touch, and a strident 'what d'you think you're doing?' was all I got for my pains. To the wonderland I had to offer, my fool preferred the corniest movies, the most cloying fudge. To think that between a Hamburger and a Humburger, she would - invariably, with an icy precision - plump for the former. Did I mention the name of that milk bar I visited a moment ago? It was, of all things, the Frigid Queen. Smiling a little sadly, I dubbed her My Frigid Princess. She did not see the wistful joke.

Oh, do not scowl at me, reader, I do not intend to convey the impression that I did not manage to be happy. Reader must understand that in the possession and thraldom of a nymphet the enchanted traveller stands, as it were, beyond happiness. For there is no other bliss on earth comparable to that of fondling a nymphet. It is hors concours, that bliss, it belongs to another class, another planet of sensitivity. Despite our tiffs, despite her nastiness, despite all the fuss and faces she made, and the vulgarity, and the danger and the horrible hopelessness of it all, I still dwelled deep in my elected paradise - a paradise whose skies were the colour of hell flames - but still a paradise.

The able psychiatrist who studied my case - and whom by now Dr Humbert has plunged, I trust, into a state of leporine fascination - is no doubt anxious to have me take my Lolita to the seaside and have me find there, at last, the 'gratification' of a lifetime urge, and release from the 'subconscious' obsession of incomplete childhood romance with the initial little Miss Lee.

Well, comrade, let me tell you that I did look for a beach though I also have to confess that by the time we reached its mirage of grey water, so many delights had already been granted me by my travelling companion that the search for a Kingdom by the Sea, a Sublimated Riviera or whatnot, far from the impulse of the subconscious, had become the rational pursuit of a purely theoretical thrill. The angels knew it, and arranged things accordingly. A visit to a plausible cove on the Atlantic side was completely messed up by foul weather. A thick damp sky, muddy waves, a sense of boundless but somehow matter-of-fact mist - what could be further removed from the crispy charm, the sapphire occasion and rosy contingency of my Riviera romance? A couple of semi-tropical beaches on the Gulf, though bright enough, were scarred and spattered by venemous beasties and swept by hurricane winds. Finally, on a Californian beach, facing the phantom of the pacific, I hit upon some rather perverse privacy in a kind of cave whence you could hear the shrieks of a lot of girl scouts taking their first surf bath on a separate part of the beach, behind rotting trees; but the fog was like a wet blanket, and the sand was gritty and clammy, and Lo was all gooseflesh and

grit, and for the first time in my life I had as little desire for her as for a manatee. Perhaps, my learned readers may perk up if I tell them that even had we discovered a piece of sympathetic seaside somewhere, it would have been too late, since my real liberation had occurred much earlier: at the moment, in point of fact, when Annabel Haze, alias Dolores Lee, alias Loleeta, had appeared to me, golden and brown, kneeling, looking up, on that shoddy veranda, in a kind of fictitious, dishonest, but eminently satisfactory seaside arrangement (although there was nothing but a second-rate lake in the neighbourhood).

So much for those special sensations, influenced, if not actually brought about, by the tenets of modern psychiatry. Consequently, I turned away - I headed my Lolita away - from beaches which were either too bleak when alone, or too populous when ablaze. However, in recollection, I suppose, of my hopeless hauntings of public parks in Europe, I was still keenly interested in outdoor activities and desirous of finding suitable playgrounds, in the open where I had suffered such shameful privations. Here, too, I was to be thwarted. The disappointment I must now register (as I gently grade my story into an expression of the continuous risk and dread that ran through my bliss) should in no way reflect on the lyrical, epic, tragic but never Arcadian American wilds. They are beautiful, heartrendingly beautiful, those wilds, with a quality of wide-eyed, unsung, innocent surrender that my lacquered, toy-bright Swiss villages and exhaustively lauded Alps no longer possess. Innumerable lovers have clipped and kissed on the trim of old-world mountainsides, on the innersprung moss, by a handy, hygienic rill, on rustic benches under the initialled oaks, and in so many cabanas in so many beech forests. But in the Wilds of America, the open-air lover will not find it easy to indulge in the most ancient of all crimes and pastimes. Poisonous plants burn his sweetheart's buttocks, nameless insects sting his; sharp items of the forest floor prick his knees, insects hers; and all around there abides a sustained rustle of potential snakes - que dis-je, of semi-extinct dragons! While the crab-like seeds of ferocious flowers cling, in a hideous green crust, to gartered dragons! While the crab-like seeds of ferocious flowers cling, in a hideous green crust, to gartered black sock and sloppy white sock alike.

I am exaggerating a little. One Summer noon, just below timberline, where heavenly-hued blossoms that I would fain call lark spur crowded all along a purly mountain brook, we did find, Lolita and I, a secluded romantic spot, a hundred feet or so above the pass where we had left our car. The slope seemed untrodden. A last painting pine was taking a well-earned breather on the rock it had reached. A marmot whistled at us and withdrew. Beneath the lap-robe I had spread for Lo, dry flowers crepitated the upper talus and a tangle of shrubs growing below us seemed to offer us protection from the sun and man alike. Alas, I had not reckoned with a faint side trail that curled up in cagey fashion among the shrubs and rocks a few feet from us. It was then that we came closer to detection than ever before, and no wonder the experience curbed for ever my yearning for rural amours.

I remember the operation was over, all over, and she was weeping in my arms - a salutary storm of sobs after one of the fits of moodiness that had become so frequent with her in the course of that otherwise admirable year! I had just retracted some silly promise she had forced me to make in a moment of blind impatient passion, and there she was sprawling and sobbing, and pinching my caressing hand, and I was laughing happily, and the atrocious, unbelievable, unbearable and, I suspect, eternal horror that I know now was still but a dot of blackness in the blue of my bliss; and so we lay, when with one of those jolts that have ended by knocking my poor heart out of its groove, I met the unblinking dark eyes of two strange and beautiful children, faunlet and nymphlet, whom their identical flat dark hair and bloodless cheeks proclaimed siblings if not twins. They stood crouching and gaping at us, both in blue playsuits, blending in with the mountain blossoms. I plucked at the lap-robe for desperate concealment - and within an instant, something that looked like a polka-dotted pushball among the undergrowth a few paces away, went into a turning motion which was transformed into the gradually rising figure of a stout lady with a raven-black bob, who automatically added a wild lily to her bouquet, while staring over her shoulder at us from behind her lovely carved bluestone children.

Now that I have an altogether different mess on my conscience, I know that I am a courageous man, but in those days I was not aware of it, and I remember being surprised by my own coolness. With the quiet murmured order one gives a sweat-stained distracted cringing trained animal even in the worst of plights (what mad hope or hate makes the young beast's flanks pulsate, what black stars pierce the heart of the tamer!), I made Lo get up and decorously walked, and then indecorously scuttled down to the car. Behind it a nifty station wagon was parked, and a handsome Assyrian with a little blue-black beard, un monsieur tres bien, in silk shirt and magenta slacks, presumably the corpulent botanist's husband, was gravely taking the picture of a sign board giving the altitude of the pass. It was well over 10,000 feet and I was quite out of breath; and with a scrunch and a skid we drove off, Lo still struggling with her clothes and swearing at me in language that I never dreamed little girls could know, let alone use.

There were other unpleasant incidents. I remember one matinee in a small airless theatre crammed with children and reeking with the hot breath of popcorn. The moon was yellow above the neckerchief crooner, and his finger was on his strumstring, and his foot was on a pine log, and I had innocently encircled Lo's shoulder and approached my jawbone to her temple, when two harpies behind us started muttering the queerest things - I do not know if I understood aright, but what I thought I did, made me withdraw my gentle hand and of course the rest of the shop was a fog to me.

Another jolt I remember is connected with a little burg we were traversing at night, during our return journey. Some twenty miles earlier I had happened to tell her that the day school she would attend at Beardsley was a rather high-class non-coeducational one, with no modern nonsense, whereupon Lo treated me to one of those furious harangues of hers where entreaty and insult, self assertion and double talk, vicious vulgarity and childish despair, were interwoven in an exasperating semblance of logic which prompted a semblance of explanation from me. En meshed in her wild words (swell chance... I'd be a sap if I took your opinion seriously... Stinker... You can't boss me... I despise you... and so forth), I drove through the slumbering town at a 50-mile-per-hour pace in continuance of my smooth highway swoosh, and a twosome of patrolmen put their spotlight on the car, and told me to pull over. I shushed Lo who was automatically raving on. The men peered at her and me with malevolent curiosity. Suddenly all dimples, she beamed sweetly at them, as she never did at my orchideous masculinity; for, in a sense, my Lo was even more scared of the law than I - and when the kind officers pardoned us and servilely we crawled on, her eyelids closed and fluttered as she mimicked limp prostration.

I now think it was a great mistake to move east again and have her go to that private school in Beardsley, instead of somehow scrambling across the Mexican border while the scrambling was good so as I could lie low for a couple of years in subtropical bliss until I could safely marry my little Creole; for I must confess that depending on the condition of my glands and ganglia, I could switch in the course of the same day from one pole of insanity to the other - from the thought that around 1950 I would have to get rid somehow of a difficult adolescent whose magic nymphage had evaporated - to the thought that with patience and luck I might have her produce eventually a nymphet with my blood in her exquisite veins, a Lolita the Second, who would be eight or nine around 1960, when I would still be dans la force de l'âge; indeed, the telescopy of my mind, or unmind, was strong enough to distinguish in the remoteness of time a vieillard encore vert - was it green rot? - bizarre, tender, salivating Dr Humbert, practising on supremely lovely Lolita the Third the art of being a grandad.

In the days of that wild journey of ours, I doubted not that as father of Lolita the First I was a ridiculous failure. I did my best; I read and reread a book with the unintentionally biblical title Know Your Own Daughter, which I got at the same store where I bought Lo, for her thirteenth birthday, a de luxe volume with commercially 'beautiful' illustrations, of Andersen's The Little Mermaid. But even at our very best moments, when we sat reading on a rainy day (Lo's glance skipping from the window to her wrist watch and back again), or had a quite hearty meal in a crowded diner, or played a childish game of cards, or went shopping or silently stared, with other motorists and their children, at some smashed, blood - bespattered car with a young woman's shoe in the ditch (Lo, as we drove on: 'That was the exact type of moccasin I was trying to describe to the jerk in the store'); on all those random occasions, I seemed to myself as implausible a father as she seemed a daughter. Was, perhaps, guilty locomotion instrumental in vitiating our powers of impersonation? Would improvement be forthcoming with a fixed domicile and a routine schoolgirl's day?

In my choice of Beardsley I was guided not only by the fact of there being a comparatively sedate school for girls located there, but also by the presence of the women's college. In my desire to get myself casé, to attach myself somehow to some patterned surface which my stripes would blend with, I thought of the man I knew in the department of French at Beardsley College; he was good enough to use my textbook in my classes and had attempted to get me over once to deliver a lecture. I had no intention of doing so, since, as I have once remarked in the course of these confessions, there are few physiques I loathe more than the heavy low-slung pelvis, thick calves and deplorable complexion of the average co-ed (in whom I see, maybe, the coffin of coarse female flesh within which my nymphets are buried alive); but as I did crave for a label, a background, and a simulacrum, and, as presently will become clear, there was a reason, a rather zany reason, why old Gaston Godin's company would be particularly safe.

Finally, there was the money question. My income was cracking under the strain of our joy-ride. True, I clung to the cheaper motor courts; but every now and then, there would be a loud hotel deluxe, or a pretentious dude ranch, to mutilate our budget; staggering sums, moreover, were expended on sightseeing and Lo's clothes, and the Old Haze bus, although a still vigorous and very devoted machine, necessitated numerous minor and major repairs. In one of our strip maps that has happened to survive among the papers which the authorities have so kindly allowed me to use for the purpose of writing my statement, I find some jottings that help me compute the following. During that extravagant year 1947-8, August to August, lodging and food cost us around $5,500; gas, oil and repairs, $1,234, and various extras almost as much; so that during about 150 days of actual motion (we covered about 27,000 miles!) plus some 200 days of interpolated standstills, this modest rentier spent around $8,000, or better say $10,000 because, unpractical as I am, I have surely forgotten a number of items.

And so we rolled East, I more devastated than braced with the satisfaction of my passion, and she glowed with health, her bi-iliac garland still as brief as a lad's, although she had added two inches to her stature and eight pounds to her weight. We had been everywhere. We had really seen nothing. And I catch myself thinking today that our long journey had only defiled with a sinuous trail of slime the lovely, trustful, dreamy, enormous country that by then, in retrospect, was no more to us than a collection of dog-eared maps, ruined tour books, old tyres, and her sobs in the night - every night, every night - the moment I feigned sleep.

REMEMBERANCE
... Lost and Found
Hubert Selby Jr

"This event is extremely important in my life and has inspired me consciously and otherwise more than I will ever know. This is where I made the decision to write, though it was about eight years before I made the commitment to writing."

He was called Hocus Pocus because he loved God. Oldest guy in the surgery ward. Thick Latvian accent, short, small hump on back, dragged his lame foot slightly like a miniature Quasi Modo.

Hocus Pocus was very attached to Alex, a young Greek boy from Egypt. In his early 20s, a year or two older than me, quiet, well mannered, liked by everyone.

Went for his first operation. Routine. Late coming back. Nurse wheeled his bedside table into her office, not down the hall to the recovery room. Somehow we all saw her. Card games stopped, radio earphones came off, newspapers, books, magazines were lowered, puzzles ignored, conversations stopped or mumbled to silence... like a freeze frame... everyone attempting to deny what they had seen, and what it meant. We remained frozen, his table glowing like neon... an eternity before Hocus Pocus hobbled to the nurse's office. Their conversation was hushed, quick, then Hocus Pocus slowly limped back to his bed, the one next to where Alex used to be, sat on his chair and cried. His sobs moved us slowly, tentatively, toward him. There were no more jokes about Hocus Pocus. No ridicule about his religious beliefs. We simply wanted to console and comfort the old man... the gentle, lonely, loving old man who had, for whatever little piece of time, found something he had been looking for that had suddenly and brutally been wrenched from him.

He sat alone for a few days, the usual hospital activity continuing around him. Then he came to my bed, his movements so painful, so labored, there did not seem to be enough time for him to walk from his bed to mine.

I jumped out of bed and pulled out the chair so he could sit. He put himself on the chair without any overt expression of pain, but there was such sadness in his movements, such a deep sense of resignation. I was just a kid yet the feelings of pain coming from the old man registered so deeply within me I carry them to this day. There is pain, sadness, and all manner of misery in this world, and there are things, experiences, feelings, so far beyond what those words imply that it is not only futile to try and describe them, but meaningless. His tearless pain was beyond despair or hopelessness. I don't know what I felt, but it seems like I had a sense of being in the presence of something far beyond my understanding, but something I instinctively knew demanded my profound respect. Today I would say I was humbled by the manner of his grieving.

He sat, folded his hands on my bed, looked at them, then looked up at me and asked me to write a letter.

I was enraged at what had happened to me, a kid once six feet tall, 175 lbs, and so arrogant he thought he was fearless. I was so pissed off I wanted to spit in the face of god. I had suffered tremendous pain physically, emotionally, psychically, and felt totally lost and trapped in a goddamn stinking world I hated with every ounce of energy I could create. My self pity was infinite yet the old man's suffering humbled me. I did not know it. Would be unaware of it all these 40 years, until this very moment, but the infinite dignity of his suffering humbled me. He was grieving the loss of something not just in his world, but in the ever so much larger world than the self centered one I was living in. I was ignorant of all this then, but he was bearing the grief of an unknown and unseen family, the tragedy of a life so shortly lived. The old man, Mr Hocus Pocus, was not wallowing in self pity, or questioning things we know nothing about, but was doing what he could to lovingly accept what was, and bring as much peace as possible to a painful situation. I did not know this then, but still my spirit was nurtured by it. Miracles are possible without my consent, and I was affected by the miracle of the old man's love, and perhaps it was that miracle that carried me through so many situations that were waiting for me. I accepted the miracle by saying yes to the old man's request. And why did he ask me to write the letter? I did not know how to write one. Why didn't he ask any of the other patients, or nurses, or aides, or doctors, or workers, or gray ladies, or even my mother? I assume because I was in greater need of the miracle he was offering than anyone else in that little world at that particular time. Now, more than 40 years later, I have a sense of that miracle... more than 40 years later. But miracles, of course, are timeless, and I am awed by what happened so long ago it was lost somewhere in my history... awed by how easily the miracle of his love found its way into my heart, and did all that it did for me, without my ever being aware of it.

He struggled to speak clearly, struggling through his accent, and grief. He asked me to write a letter and after I got paper and a pen he told me what he wanted me to write. He wanted me to write to Alex's parents and tell them that we are all sorry, and that he was a good boy. The miracle started working instantly. First it filled me with a sense of respect for the old man, got me to say yes to a request I was totally incapable of fulfilling. I did not know how to write a letter, no less the kind he wanted me to write, to people I did not know, about what has to be the greatest tragedy in a person's life... the death of their child.

I said yes and somehow wrote the letter. I have no idea what I wrote, but I realise, now, that the old man's miracle did the writing, I was incapable of writing a letter that would bring joy to the lives of Alex's family, yet that is what happened. I wrote the letter, the old man liked it, and we mailed it. In time we received a reply and the family said the letter made them very happy, that it brought much joy into their lives, and many other nice things. I remember being so overjoyed to receive their letter. I think I wrote again, once again doing the impossible.

Perhaps some day I will know just how much the old man's miracle did for me, but of far greater importance, I hope he knows what it did for me... how it helped me find something so lost I didn't know it existed... my ability to love ▮

Hubert Selby Jr is the author of Last Exit To Brooklyn and Requiem For A Dream, published by Marion Boyarf.

DICTIONARY
... Of Recieved Ideas
Gustave Flaubert

This abridged Dictionary, a separate, self-contained work within the unfinished novel Bouvard et Pecuchet, develops further the theme of human stupidity, the main drive of the book. It also includes stylistic absurdities of various kinds, as well as factual errors.
DO NOT USE THIS DOCUMENT IN AN EXAM SCENARIO.

A
AMERICA: Fine example of injustice: Columbus discovered it and it is named after Amerigo Vespucci. If it weren't for the discovery of America, we shouldn't have syphilis.
APRICOTS: 'We shan't have any again this year.'
ARCHITECTS: All idiots; they always forget to put staircases in houses.
ART: Leads to the workhouse. What use is it since machines can make things better and quicker?
ARTISTS: All charlatans. Praise their disinterestedness (old fashioned). Express surprise that they dress like everyone else (old fashioned). They earn huge sums, but squander them. Often asked to dine out. A woman artist must be a whore. What artists do can't be called work.
AUTHORS: One should 'know a few authors': no need to know their names.

B
BACK: A slap on the back could give you tuberculosis.
BALLOON: Thanks to them, man will one day reach the moon. But it will be a long time before they can be steered.
BEARD: Sign of strength. Too much beard causes baldness. Helps to protect cravats.
BLONDES: Hotter than brunettes.
BOOK: Always too long, whatever the subject.
BUSINESS: [Fr. affaires] Come first. A woman must avoid talking about hers. The most important thing in life. The be-all and end-all of existence.
BUTCHERS: Awe-inspiring in times of revolution.

C
CANNONBALL: The rush of air it creates causes blindness.
CELEBRITIES: Find out the smallest details of their private lives, so that you can run them down.
CENSORSHIP: A good thing, whatever people may say.
CHILDREN: Display a lyrical fondness for them when there are people present.
CHOLERA: You can catch it by eating melons. You cure it by drinking a lot of tea with rum in it.
CLARINET: Playing it causes blindness; all blind men play the clarinet.

COGNAC: Very harmful. Excellent for several ailments. A glass of cognac never did anybody any harm. Taken before breakfast, kills intestinal worms.

COMETS: Make fun of our ancestors who feared them.

COMFORT: Important modern discovery.

CROCODILE: Imitates the cry of a child to lure people.

D

DANCING: People don't dance any more, they walk about.

DENTURES: Third set of teeth. Take care not to swallow them while asleep.

DESSERT: Deplore the fact that people no longer sing at dessert. Virtuous persons despise it: 'Pastry! Heavens, no! I never touch it.'

DICTIONARY: Say of it; 'It's only for ignoramuses!' A rhyming dictionary? - 'I'd rather die than use one!'

DOCUMENT: Invariably 'of the highest importance'.

DUNGEON: Always horrible. The straw in it is always damp. Nobody has ever come across a delightful one.

E

EARTH: Refer to the four corners of the earth, since its round.

EDUCATION: Create the impression that you have had a good education. The common people need no education to earn their living.

ELEPHANTS: Noted for their memories, and worship the sun.

ENGLISH WOMEN: Express surprise that they can have pretty children.

ERECTION: Said only of monuments.

F

FACE: The mirror of the soul. So some people must have very ugly souls.

FAT: Fat people don't need to learn to swim. Are the despair of executioners owing to the difficulty of beheading them.

FAVOUR: It is doing children a favour to cuff them; animals, to beat them; servants, to sack them; criminals, to punish them.

FEMALE: Use only in speaking of animals. Unlike the human race, the females of animals are less beautiful than the males, *e.g.* the pheasant, the cock, the lion etc.

FEUDALISM: No need to have any clear idea what it was, but thunder against it.

FOREHEAD: High and bald, a sign of genius or of composure.

FUCK: Use this word only as a swear-word, if at all.

FULMINATE: Nice verb.

FURNITURE: Always fear the worst for your furniture.

G

GAMBLING: Wax indignant at this fatal passion.

GENIUS: No use admiring it; it's a neurosis.

GENTLEMEN: There aren't any left.

GIRAFFE: Polite word to avoid calling a woman an old cow.

GLOBE: Genteel way of referring to a woman's breasts; 'Let me kiss your adorable globes.'

GOD: Voltaire himself said; 'If God did not exist, it would be necessary to invent him.'

H

HARD: Invariably add 'as iron'. True, there is also 'hard as diamond', but that is much less forceful.

HEAT: Always 'unbearable'. Don't drink in hot weather.

HOMER: Never existed. Famous for his laughter.

HORSES: If they knew their strength, they wouldn't let themselves be led. Horsemeat: excellent subject for a pamphlet by a man who wishes to make his name. Race-horses: despise them - of what use are they?

HUMIDITY: Cause of all illness.

HUNCHBACKS: Are very witty. Much sought-after by lascivious women.

HYGIENE: Must always be carefully maintained. Prevents illnesses, except when it causes them.

I

ICE CREAM: It is dangerous to eat it.

IDEALS: Perfectly useless.

IDIOTS: Those who think differently from you.

IMAGINATION: Always 'lively'. Be on your guard against it. When you lack it, attack it in others. To write a novel, all you need is imagination.

INFINITESIMAL: Nobody knows what it means, but it has something to do with homeopathy.

INWELL: A suitable present for a doctor.

INSTRUMENT: If it has been used to commit a crime, it is always 'blunt', unless it happens to be sharp.

INTRODUCTION: Obscene word.

J

JAPAN: Everything there is made of china.

JAVELIN: As good as a gun if you know how to use it.

JEALOUSY: Always preceded by 'frantic'. Terrible passion. Eyebrows which meet in the middle are a sign of jealousy.

JUSTICE: Never worry about it.

K

KNOUT: Word which offends the Russians.

L

LABORATORY: Have one in your country house.

LADIES: Always come first. 'God bless' em!' Be careful how you use the term.

LATE: 'My late father' - and you raise your hat.

LATE NIGHTS: Are respectable in the country.

LEARNING: Despise it as the sign of a narrow mind.

LITERATURE: Occupation of idlers.

M

MAKE-UP: Ruins the skin.

MATERIALISM: Utter this word with horror, stressing each syllable.

MEDICAL STUDENTS: Sleep next to corpses. Some even eat them.

MELANCHOLY: Sign of a noble heart and a lofty mind.

MELON: Nice topic for dinner-table conversation. Is it a vegetable or a fruit? The English eat it for dessert, which is astounding.

MEMORY: Complain of your own, and indeed boast of not having any. But roar indignantly if anyone says you lack judgement.

METAPHYSICS: Laugh at it: this is proof of your superior intellect.

MILK: Dissolves oysters, attracts snakes, whitens the skin. Some women in Paris take a milk bath everyday.

MOLE: Blind as a mole. Yet moles have eyes.

MOON: Inspires melancholy. May be inhabited.

MOSQUITO: More dangerous than any wild beast.

N

NEWSPAPERS: One can't do without them, but thunder against them.

NIGHTMARES: Come from the stomach.

NINY: Never use this word in the plural when referring to a woman's breasts.

NOVELS: Corrupt the masses. Are less immoral in a serial than in volume form. Some novels are written with the point of a scalpel. Others rest on the point of a needle

O

ORGASM: Obscene term.

OSTRITCH: Can digest stones.

P

PHOTOGRAPHY: Will make painting obselete

PIG: Its insides being 'identical with those of man', they should be used in hospitals to teach anatomy.

POETRY: Completely useless and out of date.

POLICE: Always in the wrong.

PORTFOLIO: Carry one under your arm: this makes you look like a Cabinet minister.

PRIESTS: Should be castrated. Sleep with their housekeepers and give away the children whom they pass off as their nephews. Still, there are a few good ones all the same.

PRINT: One must believe whatever is in print. There are people who commit crimes just to see their name in print.

PRINTING: Wonderful invention. Has done more harm than good.

PYRAMIDE: Useless edifice.

R

RELATIVES: Always a nuisance. Keep the poor ones out of sight.

RELIGION: Part of the foundation of society. Is necessary for the common people, but there mustn't be too much of it. 'The religion of our fathers...'; this phrase must be uttered with unction.

ROPE: People don't know how strong it is – stronger than iron.

S

SCIENCE: A little science takes you away from religion; a lot brings you back to it.

SEA: Bottomless. Symbol of infinity. Inspires deep thoughts. At the seaside one should always have a telescope. While contemplating the sea always exclaim: 'Water, water everywhere!'

SELFISHNESS: Complain of other people's, and overlook your own.

SIGHT: Must be heaved near a woman.

SIGNATURE: The more ornate, the more beautiful.

SLEEP: Thickens the blood.

SNEEZE: After saying 'God bless you!' start a discussion on the origin of this custom.

STOCKBROKERS: All thieves.

SUICIDE: Proof of cowardice.

SWAN: Sings just before it dies. Can break a man's leg with its wing. The Swan of Cambrai was not a bird but a man called Fenelon. The Swan of Mantua is Virgil. The Swan of Pesaro is Rossini.

SYPHILIS: Everybody is more or less infected with it.

T

TEETH: Are spoiled by cider, tobacco, sweets, ices, drinking immediately after soup and sleeping with the mouth open. Eye-teeth: it is harmful to pull these out because they are connected with the eyes. Having a tooth out 'is no joke'.

THINKING: Painful. Things which compel us to think are generally neglected.

THIRTEEN: Avoid being thirteen at table; it brings bad luck. The sceptics should not fail to joke: 'What's the difference? I'll eat enough for two!' Or again, if there are ladies present, ask if any are pregnant.

TOBACCO: Government tobacco is not so good as that which is smuggled in. Snuff suits studious men. Cause of all the disease of the brain and spinal cord.

TOYS: Should always be educational.

U

UNPOLISHED: Whatever is antique is unpolished, and whatever is unpolished is antique. Remember this when buying antiques.

V

VELVET: On clothes, means distinction and wealth.

VOLTAIRE: Famous for his frightful rictus. His learning was superficial.

W

WAGNER: Snigger when you hear his name and joke about the music of the future.

WAR: Thunder against it.

WINE: Topic or discussion among men. The best is claret, since doctors prescribe it. The worse it tastes, the purer it is.

WOMAN: Member of the fair sex. One of Adam's ribs. Don't say 'the little woman' but 'my good lady', or, better still, 'my better half'.

WRITTEN: 'Well written'; a hall-porter's phrase to describe the newspaper serials he finds entertaining.

Y

YAWNING: Say: 'Excuse me, it isn't that I'm bored - it's my stomach.'

YOUNG GENTLEMEN: Always sowing wild oats. This is as it should be. Express astonishment when he doesn't.

YOUTH: What a wonderful thing it is! Always quote these Italian verses, even if you don't know what they mean: 'O Primavera! Gioventu!'

Translated by A J Krailsheimer
The Dictionary of Received Ideas translated by R Baldick.
Copyright © The Estate of Robert Baldick

EVERYTHINGS NARROW, SLIT, SHE DRAWS ON THE REEFER THE SM OKE CIRCLES HER FACE, FALLS THROUGH HER LIPS, FOGS HER EYES, S HE HOLDS IT IN FOREVER IN HER CHEST, LIKE THE BREATH BEFORE J UMPING OFF, SHE COMES IN FROM SOMEWHERE ELSE, HER HAIR FALLS INFR ONT OF EVERYTHING, SHE PUSHES IT BACK, LIKE SHE'S BEEN TAUGHT TO SO YOU CAN SEE HER FACE, HER LIPS. THE OTHER WAITING LIPS TOUCH. DON'T PRESS, LONGER THAN A BREATH, LONGER THAN A KISS, EYES STUCK ON EA CH OTHER, SHE PULLS BACK SLOWLY TAKING THE HIGH. THE FUMES TWIST BETWEEN THEM. SHE SUCKS ON IT TILL HOLLOW, MYSTERIOUSLY HOLDING IT INSIDE, INVISIBLY KISSING THE SMOKE BACK INTO HER MOUTH LIKE A BA CKWARDS WHISPER. SHE THROWS HER HEAD, HAIR, BACK, TAKING IT THE LAS T HEAT FUMES FROM BETWEEN HER CLOSED LIPS, LOOKING AT EACHOTHER AS HE TAKES IT AND PULLS IN THE SMOKE, THE END CANDLES, GOES OUT, SHE DRAWS IT AGAIN, IT GLOWS. THEY LEAN TOGETHER, PASSING THE SMOKE ACROSS, LINGERS, MO UTHS PRESSING, DARK BREASTS SEAMLESS, SHE PULLS AWAY, GRINNING, HOLDING IT IN HER INFLATED CHEST, SHE LAUGHS, LURCHES FORWARDS, SWIGGING FROM TH E DARK BOTTLE, HIDING THAT SHE CARES, WALKING OVER TO THE OTHERS TOSSIN G THE LIQUID DOWN HER SMOOTH ARCHED THROAT, CATCHING HER HAIR IN HER MOUTH, ITS LIKE BEING HORRIBLY CLOSE TO SOMEONE OR SOMETHING, AND ITS DARK SO YOU CANT TELL WHAT IT IS, POST COITAL, LIKE MISSING S OMETHING ABSTRACT. THE COLOR CHANGES TO FAST, EVERYTHING FAZES IN AND OUT LOOKING FOR SOMETHING TO FOCUS ON, LIKE SHE'S MATERIALISING THE GIRL COMES INTO FOCUS, CRAZY COLORS CASCADE ACROSS HER FACE SHE IS GONE IN SHADOW THEN THE SLIPPERY NEON BRINGS HER BACK, E VERYTHING FOLLOWS HER PINK EYES, LIGHT FROM SOMEWHERE ELSE REF LECTS OFF HER FACE, FLOODLIGHTS HER FLESH, SHE MOONS BEHIND THE DOORWAY SO SHE'S HIDDEN BUT CAN STILL SEE. SOMETHING'S BLOCKING THE FOREGROUN D CAN'T TELL WHAT, ITS ALL OUT OF FOCUS, FROM FURTHER BACK YOU SEE ITS A BUM, STILL BLURRY STICKING UP IN THE AIR, NAKED, BROWN AND SMOOTH, THE SKIRTS FALLING UP OVER THE GIRLS WAIST THE BREASTS HANG DOWN IN FRONT, TOUCHING HIS STOMACH, SHE MOVES, HER NIPPLE BRUSHES HIS LEG THEN HER ARM COMES FORWARDS TO GRAB ONTO HIS COCK AND YOU CANT SEE HER BREASTS ANY MORE, SHE PULLS HIS COCK UP TO HER MOUTH THEN SLID -ES DOWN ONTO IT. LIPS STRETCHED OPEN, THEN FURTHER, HER CHEEK STRETCH ED TOO. SHE PULLS OUT, THE END OF HIS COCK GLISTENING WITH HER SPIT, ITS SO LONG IT TAKES AGES TO COME OUT, SHE FALLS BACK ONTO IT, LIPS DIS APPEAR OVER IT, HE'S GONE, INTO HER, HER LONG AUBURN HAIR FALLS OVER HER LIKE FLAMES, HE JUST LIES THERE, NOTHING MOVES BUT HIS SHINING COCK AND HER FACE FALLING ONTO HIM, LETTING HIM OUT ALL THE WAY SO YOU CAN SEE HIS BURSTING NOB, SHE LICKS THE END ALL OVER LIKE SHE'S TRYING TO LICK SOMETHING OFF, LIKE A LOLLYPOP, SHE LICKS ALL THE WAY DOWN TO HIS NEAT BALLS HER CLUMSY WHITE SLING

BACKS SWING FREE. RIGHT UP CLOSE HIS FEET LOOK HUGE ALL YOU CAN SEE IS HIS SOLES AND HIS BALLS LIKE A DEAD MAN. SHE GENTLY TAKES HIS COCK IN HER HAND AND STARTS RUBBING IT INTO HER BREASTS, SIDE TO SIDE OVER HER NIPPLE, TITS SMOOTH WITH SWEAT, RUBBING FASTER HARDER, HER NIPPLE'S HARD SHE THROWS HER HEAD BACK, HER NECKLACE DANGLES DOWN ONTO HIS BALLS, HAIR STROKES HIS BELLY, HER BACK ARCHED, LEOPARD TUMMY HER LONG TRESSES ALL OVER HIM, HE PUTS HER HAND GENTLY ON HIS BUTTOCK, WHILE HE SLOWLY FINDS HER WAIST, GRABS FOR HER HAIR BUT CANT FIND IT, HER NECKLACE DANGLES DOWN ONTO HIM, EYES CLOSE, HAIR FALLING ONTO HIS BALLS. HE GRASPS FOR HER HAIR AGAIN CANT GET THERE HIS HAND HANGS IN MID AIR THEN FALLS BACK FLAT AT HIS SIDE. SHE'S STANDING UP, BIG STRAPPY FEET LIKE HOOVES, TRANSPARENT VEINS POPPING CANT TELL WHATS HAPPENING, HE LIES THERE USELESS HIS COCK STICKING UP LIKE A POLE, SHE'S STRADDLING HIM KNEE ON EITHER SIDE, SHE LEANS FORWARDS YOU CAN SEE HER CLEAN HAIRLESS ARSEHOLE BETWEEN HER BROWN BUTTOCKS, SKIRT UP AROUND HIS WAIST, COCK SHINY AND HARD IN HER HAND AS SHE GLIDES IT INTO HER CUNT, LIKE ITS MAKING ITS OWN HOLE, YOU CANT SEE HER CUNT, ITS JUST WHERE HES GOING SHE HOLDS THE SHAFT GUIDING HIM SLOWLY, LETTING IT STRETCH HER MORE, THEN HE'S IN ALL THE WAY UP TO HIS BALLS, HIS ARMS COME UP RESTING ON HIS THIGHS ROCKING HER FORWARDS AND BACK, IN AND OUT. THE SHINY EDGE OF HER CUNT AND HIS THIGHS, HER KNEES ON EITHER SIDE, SHE PUSHES HIS KNEES APART MAKING HIS COCK HERS, SHE CREEPS FURTHER ROUND THE CORNER, HER EYES WIDE, EYES LIKE SLITS. SHE LOOKS INTO HER FACE, SHE WANTS TO LOOK INTO HER PUSSY, THE GIRL LETS HER KNEES FALL APART THEN PULLS THEM TOGETHER, SHE LETS ONE FOOT DROP OFF THE EDGE MAKING HER PUSSY OPEN AND HALF PUSHES HER HEAD DOWN BETWEEN HER LEGS SHE PUSHES HER PUSSY UP A BIT SO ITS ON HER MOUTH, THE GIRL KNEELS THERE POLITELY, LIGHTLY, SUCKING HER CLIT, LOOKING UP OVER HER MINGE AT HER FACE. NOT DARING LET GO WHILE SHE STROKES AND MESSES THE CROWN OF HER HAIR, HOLDING HER IN PLACE, SHE INCHES TO THE EDGE SO SHE CAN SEE DOWN BETWEEN HER LEGS, FAINT SHE SQUEEZES THE TOP OF HER HAIR JUST TO HOLD ONTO SOMETHING, SHE CLOSES HER EYES LIKE SHE CANT TAKE IT MUCH LONGER SHE FALLS BACK AGAIN, A LINE OF SWEAT COLLECTS ON HER TUMMY, SHE WORKS HER TONGUE UP AND DOWN, ALL THE TIME WIDE SLIT EYES LOOKING IN HER FACE, THEN BURIED DOWN IN HER MINGE SO YOU CANT EVEN SEE HER NOSE OR HER FACE ANYMORE, THEN SHE PULLS BACK HANDS UNDER HER KNEES PUSHING THEM UP, PUSHING, PULLING HER OPEN SUCKING OUT HER LIPS LIKE BUTTERFLY WINGS ON EACH SIDE, SLOWLY, THE GIRL MOANS SOMETHING AND STARTS LICKING HER CUNT IN THE MIDDLE WITH VERY SHARP STROKES. THE GIRL SIGHS, DROPS HER HAND OVER THE EDGE AND GRABS THE GUYS COCK, ERECT, BOLTING SHE STARTS WANKING HIM WITHOUT EVEN LOOKING UP, SHE'S PULLING HIM BIGGER, SHE'S STILL DOWN KISSING SUCKING SPITTING ON HER STUNG CUNT, HER FACE SWEATY AND COVERED IN CUNT JUICE HAIR STUCK TO HER FOREHEAD, SHE LIGHTLY FINGERS GOLD CHAIN ROUND HER NECK, HER ARSEHOLE A BLACK DOT BETWEEN HER

OBITUARY

... "arse of the world." 1974-2001

Harmony Korine (alias Laird Henn)

Harmony Korine is the writer and director of Julien Donkey Boy and Gummo. Korine also wrote the screenplay for Larry Clarke's Kids. He is an accomplished visual artist who has exhibited internationally and is also the author of A Crack Up At the Race Riots published by Doubleday. He is currently in preproduction on his third feature film.

This world was not designed for a zebra. On the end of Henn's ability to sway his masters he was just a hermetic butterfly lover at heart who often looked after fetish zed rock tossers and militant Zionists, (especially the extremists who lived in trees and hovered on castle rooftops with rifles and army issue slingshots used primarily in target shooting illegal immigrants and all boarder crossers). Laird Henn organised himself into a bookshelf quoting grey haired horse and stallion collector. To most, Laird Henn was a dismal person to be around just ask his associates from Burbank studios, and like a pig fucker with chapped lips Henn had a zest for troubled women, women with scars, Swedish runaways, and women with damaged pride. Those he often referred to in private as "broken beuts". His first wife was the daughter of a Svengali from Tangier who made "beard soup," and had a vintage lawnmower collection and a Curtis Blow tattoo on his calf muscle. Henn made well over 30 feature films mostly dealing with misery in a world where no one cares. His work was like freebasing carpet hair. His one seminal film and winner of the Niger Negro film fest in '79 entitled "Three Blind Dice", was banned in Paris because of several references to "Gérard Depardieu's facial construct" by a beekeeper who was issued a pair of plastic tits for his title role. After the film's premiere "Three Blind Dice", was a massive hit with gays in the military and it was rumoured to be JD Salinger's last watched film before he hung himself next to a picture of Ian Curtis from Joy Division. Laird Henn believed himself no better than anyone and no worse. His films are sure to be forgotten. His novella, first published in Austria under a pseudonym became the definative text on guinea-pigs. He was rumoured to have gotten sucked off by William F Fuckly while visiting the grave of Gertrude Stein one lone Easter Sunday. When Henn had money in his pocket he would only listen to Bach's Concerto In Habitas B,C, and Wagner's magnum opus "A Pricksong For The Dead Tar Baby". When Henn was broke he would only read civil war classics and post-modern fiction that for the most part dealt in nonsense political poetry, and appropriated texts and speeches primarily those of Sir Winston Churchill and Judy Bloom's puberty prose "Magritte what's this red fluid dripping ever so thickly from my zip locked hymen?" Henn shared much in common philosophically with his favourite writer Marcel Proust. Speaking in a public debate on the value of Jane Fonda and Jean Genet, Henn was quoted as saying, "....as an artist you must live like Gatsby but think like Krishna with a 25 year addiction to cocaine and a pirated Navaho Indian teen porn collection." Henn paced all day and had frequent and often severe bouts of depression marred and tortured by insomnia. He felt as if he should have been born during the Great Depression when shrinks drank morphine tea and listened over and over to Nico records at 78rpms. Laird Henn died of a broken heart at his home on Wetback Island. Henn also made headlines during the '88 presidential election by voting for and publicly endorsing David Duke for president thinking mistakenly that he was the brother of Henn's favourite actress Patty Duke. Henn's most controversial act was when he signed a petition to legalise rape in his home state of Tennessee. In his one and only authorised bio, Memoirs Of An Amnesiac, Henn often spoke of growing up in a communal igloo with only a wine cellar and chalkboard as entertainment. After leaving "The John Burch Society Igloo Township Commune", Henn befriended famed African soccer player Pele, the two of them became roommates and lived in a Hassidic bordello on the Gaza strip called the "Wailing Ball". Henn left all his belongings to his adopted German shepherd "Klausee", who suffers both from advanced AIDS and terminal diabetes. Klausee is missing two of its legs, the front left and back right, it can't stand but it does love to eat apricots and caramel. Once Klausee barked so loud that it coughed out its own lung onto Henn's 20ft wide water bed. Laird Henn's last spoken words were a quotation from Francis Bacon that goes: "If brevity is the sole of wit, then I'll fuck handcuffs open and slash your wrists ❚❞

ELIANA WEARS **POUDRE UNIVERSEL COMPACT** IN **DORE**; EYE COLOUR **PREMIER OR LTD EDITION**; LIPSTICK **PREMIER ROUGE LTD EDITION**; BLUSH **JOUES CONTRASTE** IN **DIVINE**; EYE PENCIL **LE CRAYON YEUX** IN **BRUN**; AND **EXTREME CILS WATERPROOF MASCARA** IN **SEPIA**.

KORDA

PHOTOGRAPHY **ALBERTO KORDA**
TEXT **MARK SANDERS**
PORTRAIT **JUSTIN WESTOVER**

ALBERTO KORDA - A REVOLUTIONARY LENS

Alberto Korda, who died in Paris at the age of 72 in May of this year, was one of the undisputed masters of Cuban revolutionary photography whose iconic portrait of Che Guevara inspired a generation. Yet, before the victory of Fidel Castro's rebel army in '59, Korda was also the most famous fashion photographer in Cuba. Living the high life with a string of beautiful women and fast cars, his images of models such as Norka, rediscovered in Cuban state archives after 40 years, reveal a different side to the man whose love of beauty led to the creation of the 20th century's most effective and enduring images. Seen alongside their revolutionary counterparts they represent the missing link between Korda the fashion photographer and Korda the revolutionary photojournalist. The following interview was conducted in Havana shortly before Korda's death. As such, it stands as a testament to a man whose love of life was an inspiration to all who knew him.

The place is Havana, the year 2001, and Alberto Korda has just arisen from his afternoon nap - a Cuban custom that is non-negotiable even for Fidel Castro. Sitting in his favourite cane chair with the late afternoon sun casting shadows across his face, he sips slowly from a glass of Cuba Libre while taking long and considered draws on his filterless Cuban cigarettes. Plumes of smoke drift from his mouth and float listlessly out across the balcony before descending into the busy street below. Korda is now deep in thought. His piercing eyes, the very embodiment of youth, reveal a passion for life that has never left him. Recollecting the day, 1) before the Revolution, that he first met the 18-year-old model Norka, the young girl whose face he immortalised in the mid '50s and who later become his wife, Korda smiles gently to himself. "When I first saw her she was incredibly shy, hiding her face against the wall", he declares, describing the event as if it was only yesterday. "I took one photograph of her and realised that she was the woman I was looking for."

This was the Havana of the '50s and Korda was at the height of his career as a fashion photographer. His studio, known simply as "The Korda Studio", had been opened in '56 and, within a year of that date, had become the city's leading fashion centre. Yet by the end of the decade, Korda's camera would be employed in the service of a very different kind of beauty, his love of romance and idealism embodied in the splendour of the Revolution. "A man who develops a work like mine is dedicated to something that he loves," Korda explains passionately. "I did that from the very beginning. I have loved the beauty of women as much as the beauty of the men who led the Revolution. The beauty of those men is not only aesthetic but also moral. Loving as I did the work that I made with men like Fidel Castro and Che Guevara, you can see the similarities between both types of photography: fashion and revolutionary."

It was early on the morning of January 8, 1959 that Fidel Castro, at the head of his rebel army, entered Cuba's capital Havana. For seven years, the country had been under the shadow

1

of a military dictatorship led by General Fulgencio Batista. In the months preceding the coup, Cuba had been gripped by mounting civil unrest and general strikes occurred with increasing regularity. Thousands of Cuban civilians lost their lives in the struggle for liberation, and it is hard to imagine the impact that Castro's victory had on ordinary Cuban citizens. Fidel and his fellow *barbudos* (bearded ones) represented radical change and new hope for the future. They symbolised the triumph of idealism over corruption and the revolutionary power of youth to mould and construct a collective future. Korda, a young man of the same generation as Fidel, immediately identified with the rebels and recognised the photographic possibilities offered by the Revolution. Endowed with a keen photographic eye, he immediately made the link between fashion photography and the revolutionary aesthetic. "That moment was a revelation to me," Korda remembers fondly. "As every man from Havana, known as *los Habaneros*, I awaited the arrival of Fidel and the *los barbudos* on January 8. Those men that came from the Sierra Maestra were young and beautiful, just like my models."

Of all the revolutionaries that entered Havana that day, the most impressive and charismatic was undoubtedly the young Argentine doctor, Ernesto "Che" Guevara. A Comandante of the rebel armed forces, and second only to Fidel Castro and his brother Raul in the rebel hierarchy, he was the archetypal revolutionary hero. Young, good looking and with a passion for social justice, his face embodied the idealism of youth and revolutionary ardour. Just one year after the rebel victory, Korda recorded the image of that face. An image that has today become one of the most famous and iconic photographic images in history. Taken during a political rally to mourn the victims of La Coubre (a Belgian ship that had exploded in the main port of Havana in >

3

STOCKISTS 2\2

JILL STUART
New York (+1)212 343 2300

JODY BUSBY JEWELLERY
London YASMIN CHO (+44)20 7482 5561
New York BARNEYS (+1)212 826 8900

JUNYA WATANABE
London COMME DES GARÇONS
(+44)20 7493 1258
Paris (+33)1 43 27 30 30
New York (+1)212 604 9200
Milan (+39)02 65 92 01 5

KATAYONE ADELI
London HARVEY NICHOLS (+44)20 7235 5000
New York (+1)212 260 3500

KENI VALENTI
New York (+1)212 967 7147

LANCÔME
Department stores nationwide

LAURENCE STEELE
London SELFRIDGES (+44)20 7629 1234
Paris ZAPATA EMILIANO (+33)1 47 05 42 09
New York JEFFREY (+1)212 206 1272

LEVI'S
London (+44)20 7292 2500
Paris (+33)1 48 28 49 36
New York (+1)212 826 5957
Milan D.SLY (+39)02 89 42 31 78

LINDA CANTELLO COSMETICS
London SPACE NK (+44)20 7379 7030
Enquiries (+1)212 829 1111

LONSDALE
London (+44)20 7434 1741
Paris (+33)1 45 79 83 57

LOEWE
London (+44)20 7493 3914
Paris (+33)1 53 57 92 50
New York BERGDORF GOODMAN
(+1)212 753 7300

LOUIS VUITTON
London (+44)20 7399 4050
Paris (+33)1 08 10 81 00 10
New York (+1)212 886 VUITTON
Milan (+39)02 77 71 71 1

LULU GUINNESS
London (+44)20 7823 4828
Paris VICTOIRE (+33)1 45 44 28 14
New York BOND 7 (+1)212 677 8487
Milan (+39)02 76 00 13 09

MARC BY MARC JACOBS
London HARVEY NICHOLS (+44)20 7235 5000
New York BERGDORF GOODMAN
(+1)212 753 7300

MARC JACOBS
London HARVEY NICHOLS (+44)20 7235 5000
Paris MARIA LUISA (+33)1 47 03 96 15
New York (+1)212 343 1490
Milan (+39)02 76 00 46 09

MARC JACOBS MEN
New York (+1)646 638 1185

MARCUS CONSTABLE
London WHISTLES (+44)20 7487 4484
Boston LOUIS (+1)617 262 6100

MARKS & SPENCER
London Marble Arch (+44)20 7935 7954
Paris (+33)1 47 42 42 91
New York (+1)212 267 2400

MARNI
London (+44)20 7235 1991
Paris COLETTE (+33)1 55 35 33 90
New York BERGDORF GOODMAN
(+1)212 753 7300
Milan (+39)02 76 31 73 27

MARTIN MARGIELA
London BROWNS (+44)20 7491 7833
Paris LE PRINTEMPS (+33)1 42 82 50 00
New York BARNEYS (+1)212 450 8307

MATTHEW WILLIAMSON
London HARVEY NICHOLS (+44)20 7813 2385
Paris COLETTE (+33)1 55 35 33 90
New York KIRNA ZABETTE (+1)212 352 9905

MATT MADE IN THE USA
New York BARNEYS (+1)212 826 8900
Enquiries (+1)212 925 9700

MARIA
New York (+1)212 643 4810

MENDED VEIL
London YASMIN CHO (+44)20 7482 5561
New York BARNEYS (+1)212 450 8307

MICHAEL AND HUSHI
New York (+1)212 253 8719

MIGUEL ADROVER
London KOH SAMUI (+44)20 7836 9434
Paris (+33)1 47 20 21 11
New York JEFFREY (+1)212 206 1272
Milan DIECI CORSO COMO (+39)02 29 00 26 74

MISSONI
London HARVEY NICHOLS (+44)20 7813 2385
Paris (+33)1 45 48 38 02
New York (+1)212 517 9339
Milan (+39)02 76 00 14 79

MIU MIU
London (+44)20 7409 0900
Paris (+33)1 53 63 20 30
New York (+1)212 334 5156
Milan (+39)02 76 00 17 99

MOSCHINO
London (+44)20 7318 0555
Paris CARRE (+33)1 42 60 08 69
New York (+1)212 639 9600
Milan (+39)02 76 00 08 32

NARCISO RODRIGUEZ
New York BARNEYS (+1)212 826 8900
Milan (+39)02 76 31 70 72

NIKE
London (+44)20 7612 0800
Paris (+33)1 42 72 38 61
New York (+1)212 891 6453
Italy (+39)01 65 77 51 49

NICOLE FARHI
London (+44)20 7499 8368
New York (+1)212 223 8811

NINA RICCI MEN
Paris (+33)1 49 52 57 35
New York JIMMY'S (+1)718 645 7873
Milan PANDA DI ANTONELLA
(+39)02 89 40 82 67

O'NEILL
London (+44)20 7836 7686
Los Angeles (+1)318 324 0204

ORFI
Enquiries (+1)212 625 9657

PACO RABANNE
Enquiries (+33)1 45 48 82 26

PATRICK COX
Enquiries (+44)20 7730 8886

PAUL SMITH
London (+44)20 7379 7133
Paris (+33)1 42 84 15 30
New York (+1)212 627 9770\1
Milan (+39)02 58 31 65 02

PIERRE CARDIN
Enquiries (+33)1 42 66 92 25

PLEIN SUD
Enquiries (+33)1 49 29 71 59

POLO RALPH LAUREN
London (+44)20 7535 4600
Paris (+33)1 44 77 53 00
New York (+1)212 650 4438

PRADA
London (+44)20 7647 5000
Paris (+33)1 45 48 53 14
New York (+1)212 664 0010
Milan (+39)02 77 71 77 1

PRINGLE SCOTLAND
London (+44)20 7470 8600
UK enquiries 0800 360 200

QUIKSILVER
London (+44)20 7836 5371
New York (+1)212 334 4500

RAF SIMONS
London THE PINEAL EYE (+44)20 7434 2567
Paris COLETTE (+33)1 55 35 33 90
New York BARNEYS (+1)212 450 8307
Milan DIECI CORSO COMO (+39)02 29 00 26 74

RALPH LAUREN
London (+44)20 7535 4600
Paris (+33)1 44 77 53 00
New York (+1)212 650 4438

RESURRECTION
New York (+1)212 228 0063

RUSSELL SAGE
London YASMIN CHO (+44)20 7482 5561
New York HENRI BENDEL (+1)212 247 1100
Enquiries (+44)20 8533 4102

SOPHIA KOKOSALAKI
London SOMETHING (+44)20 7299 9944
New York HENRI BENDEL (+1)212 247 1100
Paris BEAUTY BY ET VOUS (+33)1 47 42 30 48
Milan LINK SRL (+39)02 55 23 03 14

SPEEDO
Enquiries (+44)115 910 5267

THE GIRL CAN'T HELP IT
London (+44)20 7724 8984

TAWFIK MONNAYER
tawfikmonnayer.com

**TOM FORD FOR YVES SAINT
LAURENT RIVE GAUCHE**
London (+44)20 7235 6706
Paris (+33)1 42 65 74 59
New York (+1)212 988 3821
Milan (+39)02 76 00 05 73

TOMMY HILFIGER
London (+44)20 7235 2500
Paris GALLERIES LAFAYETTE (+33)1 42 82 34 56
New York (+1)212 548 1000

TRICKERS
London (+44)20 7930 6395

TRUSSARDI
Enquiries (+39)02 76 00 00 64

UNITED BAMBOO
London LIBERTY (+44)20 7734 1234
New York BARNEYS (+1)212 450 8307

VALENTINO
London SELFRIDGES (+44)20 7629 1234
Paris (+33)1 47 23 64 61
New York (+1)212 223 4646
Milan (+39)02 76 00 64 78

VERSACE
London (+44)20 7499 1862
Paris (+33)1 47 42 88 02
New York (+1)212 744 5572
Milan (+39)02 76 00 85 28

VERSUS
London (+44)20 7355 2700
Paris (+33)1 45 49 22 66
New York (+1)212 744 6868
Milan (+39)02 76 01 49 24

VICINI
London HARVEY NICHOLS (+44)20 7813 2385
New York (+1)212 245 3674
Milan (+39)02 76 00 28 28

VIKTOR & ROLF
London THE PINEAL EYE (+44)20 7434 2567
Paris COLETTE (+33)1 55 35 33 90

VIRGINIA
London (+44)20 7727 9908

**VIVIENNE WESTWOOD \
VIVIENNE WESTWOOD MAN**
London (+44)20 7439 1109
Paris (+33)1 49 27 01 92
New York (+1)212 334 1500
Milan (+39)02 76 39 54 97

WARREN NORONHA
London SOMETHING (+44)20 7299 9944
New York HENRI BENDEL (+1)212 373 6313

WILLIAM REID
London YASMIN CHO (+44)20 7482 5561

YOHJI YAMAMOTO
London (+44)20 7491 4129
Paris (+33)1 45 08 82 45
New York (+1)212 966 9066

Y'S FOR MEN BY YOHJI YAMAMOTO
London HARVEY NICHOLS (+44)20 7235 5000
Paris (+33)1 42 21 42 93
Milan (+39)02 29 00 26 74

ZINCO
Enquiries (+39)05 18 62 04 79 9

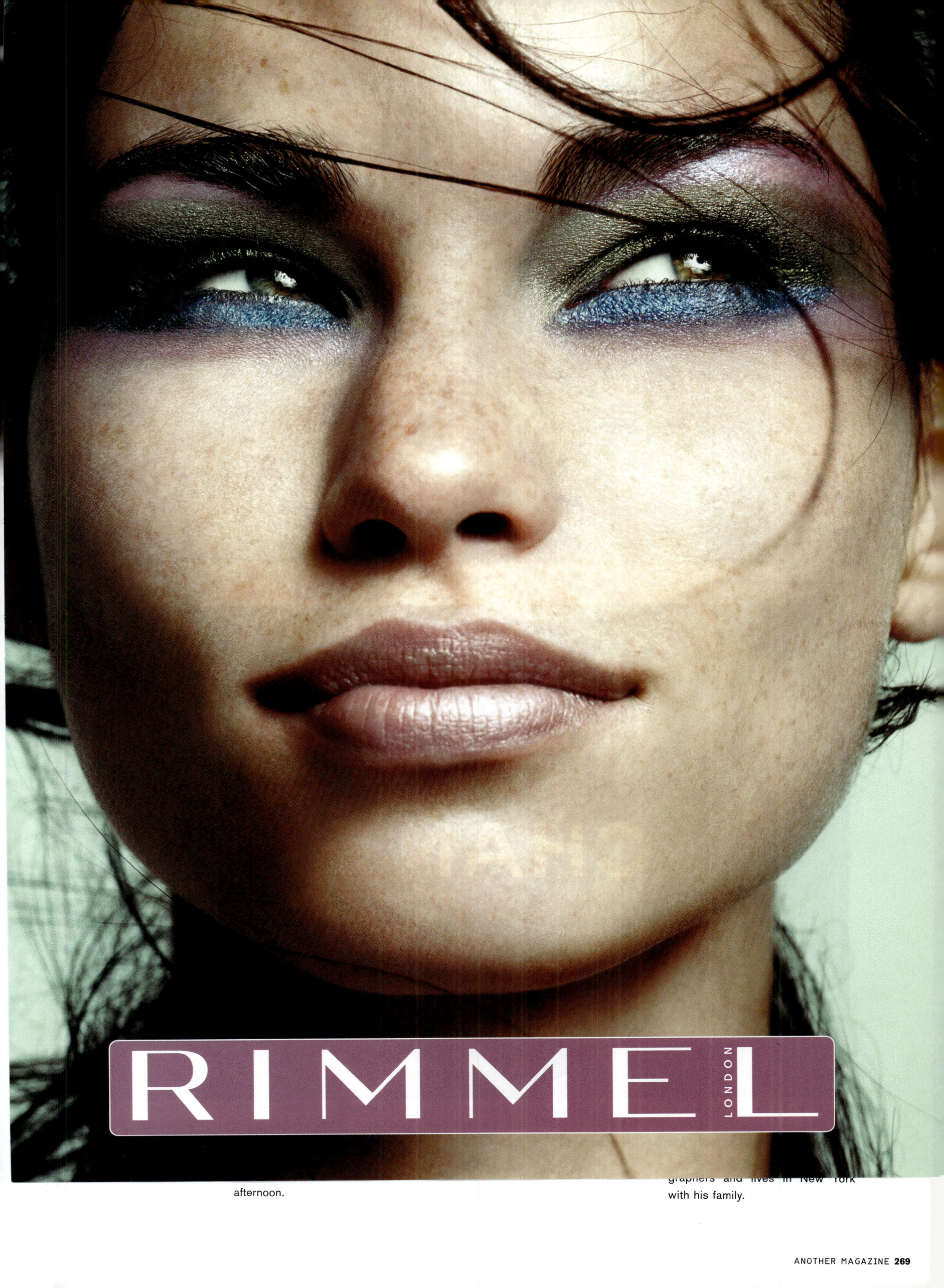

RIMMEL LONDON

afternoon.

graphers and lives in New York with his family.

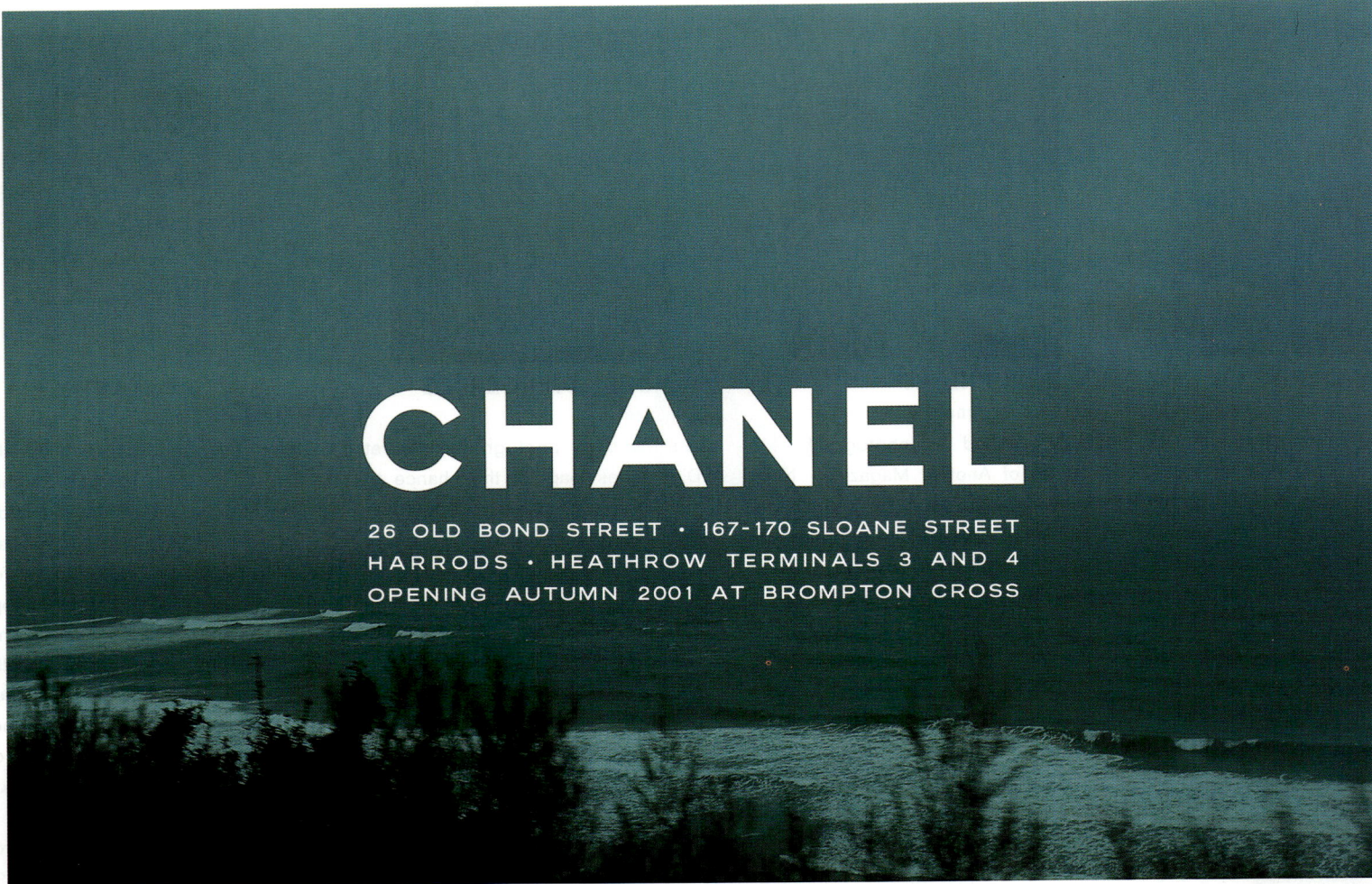

CHANEL

26 OLD BOND STREET · 167-170 SLOANE STREET
HARRODS · HEATHROW TERMINALS 3 AND 4
OPENING AUTUMN 2001 AT BROMPTON CROSS

INDEX

AD - Another Document